STORYFUN 1

T0349622

TEACHER'S BOOK

Second edition

Karen Saxby
Lucy Frino

Cambridge University Press
www.cambridge.org/elt

Cambridge Assessment English
www.cambridgeenglish.org

Information on this title: www.cambridge.org/9781316617069

© Cambridge University Press 2017

It is normally necessary for written permission for copying to be obtained in advance from a publisher. The worksheets, role-play cards, tests and tapescripts at the back of this book are designed to be copied and distributed in class. The normal requirements are waived here and it is not necessary to write to Cambridge University Press for permission for an individual teacher to make copies for use within his or her own classroom. Only those pages which carry the wording **'PHOTOCOPIABLE © Cambridge University Press 2017'** may be copied.

First published 2011
Second edition 2017

20 19 18 17 16 15 14 13 12 11 10 9 8 7

Printed in Great Britain by CPI Group (UK) Ltd, Croydon CR0 4YY

A catalogue record for this publication is available from the British Library

ISBN 978-1-316-61701-4 Student's Book with online activities and Home Fun booklet 1
ISBN 978-1-316-61706-9 Teacher's Book with Audio 1

Cambridge University Press has no responsibility for the persistence or accuracy of URLs for external or third-party internet websites referred to in this publication, and does not guarantee that any content on such websites is, or will remain, accurate or appropriate. Information regarding prices, travel timetables and other factual information given in this work is correct at the time of first printing but Cambridge University Press does not guarantee the accuracy of such information thereafter.

Contents

☆ = Value	🔊 = Let's say! pages
♪ = Song	▶ = Audio
➜ = Practice for Starters	IA = Interactive activity
✳ = Let's have fun! pages	🏠 = Home FUN booklet
💬 = Let's speak! pages	👆 = Online activities

Introduction

Welcome to *Storyfun*!

Storyfun is a series of six books written for young learners aged between 6 and 12 years. The series provides story-based preparation for the Cambridge English: Young Learners tests (YLE). Each Student's Book contains eight stories with activities that include vocabulary and grammar tasks, puzzles, games, poems, songs and an exploration of the story 'value' (for example, an appreciation of nature, the importance of friendship). The Teacher's Books provide detailed suggestions on how to approach the storytelling, together with clear instructions for guiding learners through the unit. With a variety of flexible resources, each unit in *Storyfun* is designed to provide approximately three to four hours of class time.

Why stories?

Storyfun aims to provide an opportunity for language practice by engaging learners' interest in stories.

Research has shown that meaningful and imaginative stories can motivate learning because learners:
o   engage with the text and their imaginations.
o   learn vocabulary with repetition of key words in the text and pictures.
o   are exposed to repeated rhyme and sound patterns and accurate pronunciation.
o   develop deeper social understanding by relating to characters and events in the story.
o   actively engage listening skills as they predict, hypothesise and await outcomes.

Points to remember for effective learning:
o   Story-reading should be interactive (teacher and learners). It should involve pointing, describing and discussing how the story relates to the real world.
o   Learners will engage with a story more if they are encouraged to 'work out' the meaning, for example, why learners think characters did something or how characters felt at a certain moment and, of course, what the story 'value' is.
o   Learners benefit from more than one reading or hearing of a story. At least one reading should be read/heard right the way through from beginning to end without interruption.

For more information about stories in language learning, go to.

Why Cambridge English: Young Learners (YLE)?

The stories have been written to reflect the different language levels and topic areas of the Cambridge English: Starters, Movers and Flyers tests and to appeal to the target-reader age groups. The language of the stories is exploited in activities that check comprehension, teach key vocabulary and grammar, practise all four language skills (reading, writing, listening and speaking) and give learners an opportunity to familiarise themselves with the nature and format of the Cambridge English: Young Learners tests. The optional *Let's have fun!* and *Let's speak!* sections at the back of the books also provide opportunities for collaborative learning and test speaking practice. The *Let's say!* pages support early pronunciation skills, building from sounds to sentences.

There are two Student's Books for each test: pre-A1 (Starters), A1 (Movers) and A2 (Flyers). Storyfun 1 gently introduces students to the Cambridge English: Starters language and topics through fun activities and test-style practice. Activities are carefully graded to ensure learners are guided towards the test level, with frequent opportunities to build up their language and skills. Storyfun 2 provides full examples of all the Cambridge English: Starters test tasks. By the end of Storyfun levels 1 and 2, constant recycling of language and test task types ensures learners are fully prepared for the Cambridge English: Starters test.

Who is *Storyfun* for?

Storyfun has been written for teachers and young learners of English in a wide variety of situations. It is suitable for:
o   learners in this age group who enjoy reading and listening to stories
o   large and small groups of learners
o   monolingual and multilingual classes
o   learners who are beginning preparation for the Cambridge English: Starters test
o   young learners who need to develop their vocabulary, grammar and language
o   young learners keen to discuss social values, develop collaborative learning skills and build confidence for the Starters Speaking paper
o   teachers who wish to develop their learners' literacy skills

What are the key features of *Storyfun*?

Student's Book
o   eight imaginative and motivating stories
o   fun, interactive, creative and meaningful activities
o   activities similar to task types found in all three parts (Reading and Writing, Listening and Speaking) of the Cambridge English: Starters test

- o an introduction to Cambridge English: Starters grammar and vocabulary
- o extension activities *Let's have fun!*, further speaking practice *Let's speak!* and an early pronunciation focus *Let's say!*
- o a unit-by-unit word list

Home FUN Booklet

- o fun activities for learners to try at home
- o 'self-assessment' activities that build learners' confidence and encourage autonomy
- o a Cambridge English: Starters picture dictionary
- o *Let's have fun!* pages to encourage learners to use English in the wider world
- o answers, audio and additional support found online by using the access code at the front of the book

Teacher's Book with Audio

- o a map of the Student's Book (topics, grammar points and Starters test practice for each unit)
- o practical step-by-step notes with suggestions for:

  - ✓ personalisation at presentation and practice stages
  - ✓ skills work: reading, writing, listening, speaking, drawing and colouring
  - ✓ pair and group work
  - ✓ puzzles, games, poems and songs
  - ✓ speaking activities and projects
  - ✓ discussion tasks to explore the story 'value'
  - ✓ recycling of language
  - ✓ incorporating digital materials into the lesson

- o Cambridge English: Starters test tips
- o full audioscripts
- o imaginative audio recordings for stories and activities (downloadable by using the access code at the front of this book) reflective of the Cambridge English: Starters Listening test.
- o photocopiable pages for the Student's Book or optional extension activities
- o links to online practice and the Home FUN booklet

Presentation plus

- o digital version of all Student's Book pages
- o interactive Student's Book activities
- o audio played directly from the digital page
- o digital flashcards with audio
- o digital slideshow of every story
- o an Image carousel that provides further visuals associated with story themes
- o integrated tools to make notes and highlight activities

Online Practice

For the Teacher
- o Presentation plus
- o All audio recordings
- o Additional digital resources to support your classes

For the Student
- o Fun activities to practise the exam, skills and language
- o All audio recordings
- o Additional digital resources

Word FUN World App

- o Cambridge English: Young Learners vocabulary game
- o For mobile phones and tablets

Storytelling

Why should we use stories in language learning classes?

There are several reasons! A good story encourages us to turn the next page and read more. We want to find out what happens next and what the main characters do and say to each other. We may feel excited, sad, afraid, angry or really happy. The experience of reading or listening to a story is likely to make us 'feel' that we are part of the story, too. Just like in our 'real' lives, we might love or hate different characters. Perhaps we recognise ourselves or other people we know in some of the story characters. Perhaps they have similar talents, ambitions, weaknesses or problems.

Because of this natural connection with story characters, our brains process the reading of stories differently from the way we read factual information. This is because our brains don't always recognise the difference between an imagined situation and a real one so the characters become 'alive' to us. What they say or do is therefore <u>much more meaningful</u>. The words and structures that relate a story's events, descriptions and conversations are processed by learners in a deeper way.

Encouraging learners to read or listen to stories should therefore help them to learn a second language in a way that is not only fun, but memorable.

How else do stories help?

Stories don't only offer the young reader a chance to learn more vocabulary and develop their grammatical skills. The experience also creates an opportunity to develop critical and creative thinking, emotional literacy and social skills. As learners read a story, they will be imagining far more details than its words communicate. Each learner will, subconsciously, be 'animating' the characters and making judgements and predictions about events.

As a teacher, you can encourage creativity and critical thinking by asking learners in groups to develop characters in more detail, talk about the part of the story they enjoyed most/least or even write different endings. You can also discuss, in English or L1 if necessary, the story 'values', in other words, what different stories teach us about how to relate to others.

Stories also offer a forum for personalised learning. No two learners will feel exactly the same about a story and an acceptance of difference can also be interesting to explore and discuss in class.

How can we encourage learners to join in and ask parents to help?

If, at first, learners lack confidence or motivation to read stories in English, help by reading the story to them without stopping so learners are just enjoying the story, stress free, and following as well as they can by looking at the pictures. During a second reading you might encourage interaction by asking questions like *Is this funny, scary or sad?* (Starters) *Was that a good idea?* (Movers) *What do you think will happen next?* (Flyers). If the class is read to in a relaxed and fun way, learners will subconsciously relate to the reading and language learning process more confidently and positively. Of course, being read to by a parent at home, too, is also simply a lovely way to share quiet and close time. To engage parents in the language learning process, you might share some of the above points with them or encourage them to search online for language learning activities to do at home with their children.

The Home FUN booklet has been specially designed for learners to use at home with parents. Activities are fun and easy to follow, requiring little instruction. The booklet aims to help learners show parents what they have learnt at school and to engage them in the learning process.

Further suggestions for storytelling

o Involve learners in the topic and ask guessing and prediction questions in L1 if necessary. This will engage learners in the process of storytelling and motivate learning. When you pause the audio during the story, ask learners …

  ➤ about the topic and themselves
  ➤ to guess aspects of the story
  ➤ to say how they think a character feels or what they may say next

o If you are telling the story yourself, support your learners in any way you can by adding your own dramatisation. For instance, you can read the stories with as much animation as possible and use props such as puppets or soft toys and different voices to bring the stories to life.

o Incorporate the use of realia into the storytelling process. For example, if you are using *Storyfun 1*, in 'Kim's birthday' you could set up the classroom to look like a party with balloons, cards and presents, and in 'Let's go there now' you could bring different sports equipment into the classroom to use.

o Once learners are familiar with the story they could even act out parts of the story in role plays. This will not only involve learners in the stories and add a fun element but can also help in practising and consolidating language.

Suggestions for using the story pictures

For skills practice

o Before listening to the story, learners look at all the pictures on the story pages and discuss in small groups who or what they think the story is about and what are the key events.

o Learners trace a picture (adding their own choice of extra details) and then follow your colouring or drawing instructions.

To encourage creative thinking

o Groups choose two people in a picture and imagine what they are saying to each other. They then write a question with answer or a short dialogue.

o Groups choose a background person in a picture and invent details about him/her. For example, how old they are, what they like doing, where they live, what pet they have.

o Groups invent details that are unseen in the picture, for example, ten things in a bag, cupboard or garden.

o Learners imagine they are 'in' the picture. What is behind / in front of / next to them? What can they feel (the sun, a cold wind …), smell (flowers, cooking …) or hear (birds, traffic …)?

To revise vocabulary and grammar

o Learners find as many things in a picture as they can which begin with a particular letter, for example, f.

o Learners list things in a picture that are a certain colour or place. For example, what someone is wearing or what is on the table.

o Learners choose four things they can see in a picture and list the words according to the size of the object or length of the word. Learners could also choose things according to categories such as food or animals.

o Using the pictures to revise grammar, for example *This is / These are*.

o Choose a picture in the story and ask learners in groups to say what is happening in this part of the story.

o Practise prepositions by asking learners what they can see in a picture in different places, for example, in the box, on the table or under the tree.

o Practise question forms by asking learners about different aspects of a picture, for example: *What colour is the cat? How many ducks are there? What's the boy doing?*

o On the board, write the first and last letter of four things learners can remember in a particular story picture. Learners complete the words.

o Point to objects or people in a picture and ask *This/These yes/no* questions. For example: *Is this a shoe? Are these toys? Is this a boy? Are these hats?*

o Ask *yes/no* colour and *how many* questions. For example, point to an apple and ask *Is this apple blue? Can you see four apples?*

o Show learners a story picture for 30 seconds and then ask *What's in that picture?* Write learners' answers on the board.

o Ask simple 'What's the word' questions and build on known vocabulary sets. For example: *It's green. You can eat it. It's a fruit.* (a pear / an apple / a grape / a kiwi)

Suggestions for using the word list

At the back of the Student's Book, learners will find a list of important Starters words that appear in each unit.

o Play 'Which word am I?' Learners work in pairs, looking at the word list for the unit. Choose a noun and give the class clues about it until one pair guesses it. Don't make the clues too easy and focus on form first and meaning afterwards. Say, for example: *I've got four letters. The letter 'k' is in me. You can sit on me. You can ride me to school.* (bike)

o Divide the class into A and B pairs. Learner A sits facing the board. Learner B sits with his/her back to the board. Write four words (nouns or verbs are best) from the word list for the unit on the board. Learner A then draws or mimes them until their partner guesses them all and writes them correctly (with the help of Learner A who can only say *Yes, that's right!* or *No, that's wrong!*). When everyone has finished, learners change places. Write some new words on the board. Learner B in each pair mimes these words for Learner A to guess.

o Play 'Tell me more, please!' Choose a noun from the word list for the unit and write it on the board, for example: banana. Learners take turns to add more information about the banana. For example, Learner A says: The banana is long. Learner B adds: The banana is long. It's yellow. Learner C says: The banana is long. It's yellow. It's a fruit. Continue until learners can't remember previous information.

o Pairs work together to make as many words from the word list for the unit as they can, using a number of letters that you dictate to the class. Alternatively, use word tiles from board games or letter cards made by the class. These could also be used for spelling tests in pairs or groups.

o On the board, write eight words from the word list for the unit with the letters jumbled. Pairs work as fast as they can to find the words and spell them correctly.

o On the board, write eight words from the word list for the unit. Spell three or four of them incorrectly. Pairs work as fast as they can to identify the misspelt words (they shouldn't be told how many there are) and to write them down correctly.

o Play 'Make a word'. Each group chooses a word (four, five or six letters long) from the word list for the unit and creates it by forming a human sculpture, i.e. learners in each group stand in a line, using their arms or legs to create the shapes of each letter. Remember you may need two learners for some letters (e.g. k). When all the groups are ready, the words are guessed.

o Use the word list for the unit to play common word games such as hangman, bingo and definition games or for dictated spelling tests. A common alternative to the traditional hangman, which learners may enjoy, is an animal with its mouth open, with 8–10 steps leading down into its mouth. (You could use a crocodile at Starters, a shark at Movers or a dinosaur at Flyers.) With each incorrect guess, the stick person falls down onto the next step, and gets eaten if they reach the animal's mouth!

For more information on Cambridge English: Young Learners, please visit. From here, you can download the handbook for teachers, which includes information about each level of the Young Learners tests. You can also find information for candidates and their parents, including links to videos of the Speaking test at each level. There are also sample test papers, as well as further games and songs and links to the Teaching Support website.

A few final classroom points

Please try to be as encouraging as possible when working through the activities. By using phrases such as *Now you! You choose! Well done! Don't worry!* (all on the Starters word list) you are also helping learners to feel more confident about participating fully in the class and trying hard to do their best. Make sure that everyone in your class adds to open class work, however minimally, and when mistakes are made, view them as opportunities for learning. Try not to interrupt to correct learners during open class discussion, role plays, etc. Doing so might negatively affect a child's willingness to contribute in future. It takes courage to speak out in class. Make mental notes of mistakes and then cover them at a later moment with the whole class.

Have fun!

But most of all, please remember that an hour's lesson can feel very much longer than that to a learner who feels excluded, fearful of making mistakes, unsure about what to do, unable to follow instructions or express any personal opinions. An hour's lesson will feel like five minutes if a learner is having fun, sensing their own progress and participating fully in enjoyable and meaningful activities.

How is the Student's Book organised?

Story

Four illustrated story pages using language (topics, vocabulary and grammar) needed for the Cambridge English: Starters test.

Vocabulary activity

Each unit of four-page activities opens with a vocabulary comprehension activity related to the key Cambridge English: Starters vocabulary presented in the story.

Value key phrase

A key English phrase in a speech bubble (sometimes in bold) within the story demonstrates the story 'value'. For example, *Appreciating differences and similarities* → "Do you like …? Yes, I do. / No, I don't."

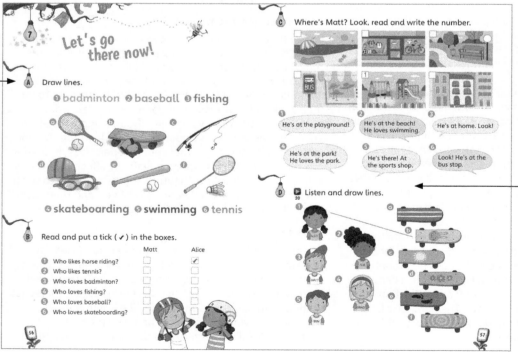

Practice for Starters activities

gently introduce learners to the style of the Cambridge English: Starters test tasks and cover the key skills, vocabulary and grammar necessary for the test. See ➡ in the Teacher's Book for identification.

Skills

All activities develop reading, writing, listening and speaking skills useful for the YL tests.

♪ Songs

Open activities such as poems and songs maintain learners' motivation and interest.

Value activities encourage learners to think about the story in a social context and practise the key phrase. The phrase aids learners to contextualise, remember and demonstrate the value in English.

✤ **Let's have fun!** ○
Optional projects or games at the back of the Student's Book promote collaborative learning.

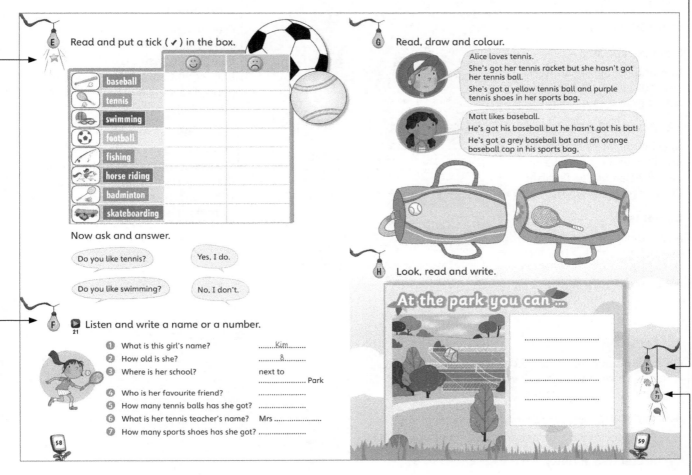

E Read and put a tick (✔) in the box.

	😊	😞
baseball		
tennis		
swimming		
football		
fishing		
horse riding		
badminton		
skateboarding		

Now ask and answer.

Do you like tennis?   Yes, I do.

Do you like swimming?   No, I don't.

F ▶ Listen and write a name or a number.
21

1 What is this girl's name? ....Kim........
2 How old is she? ....8........
3 Where is her school? next to .... Park
4 Who is her favourite friend? ....
5 How many tennis balls has she got? ....
6 What is her tennis teacher's name? Mrs ....
7 How many sports shoes has she got? ....

58

G Read, draw and colour.

Alice loves tennis.
She's got her tennis racket but she hasn't got her tennis ball.
She's got a yellow tennis ball and purple tennis shoes in her sports bag.

Matt likes baseball.
He's got his baseball but he hasn't got his bat!
He's got a grey baseball bat and an orange baseball cap in his sports bag.

H Look, read and write.

At the park you can ...

p. 71

p. 73

59

▶ Accompanying audio tracks can be found on Presentation plus or online.

💬 **Let's speak!** ○
Optional extra speaking practice at the back of the Student's Book allows learners to practise the language needed for the speaking part of the Cambridge English: Starters test.

🔊 ▶ **Let's say!** Optional pronunciation practice at the back of the Student's Book focusses on initial key sounds to develop early speaking skills. Supported by accompanying audio.

How could teachers use *Storyfun 1*?

1 Encourage learners to predict the general topic of the story using flashcards and the story pictures.
2 Teach or revise any Cambridge English: Starters words that are important in the story.
3 Play the audio or read the story.
4 (Optional) Discuss the story 'value' with learners. You will probably need to do this in your learners' first language to fully explore what the story teaches the reader.
5 Present the vocabulary and general comprehension tasks (usually Activities A–C).
6 Present the grammar, vocabulary and skills sections (generally Activities D–H).
7 Encourage collaborative learning with the 'Let's have fun!' at the back of the Student's Book.
8 Follow communicative pair or group work suggestions in the 'Let's speak!' pages at the back of the Student's Book.
9 Use extension activities in the Teacher's Books or set homework tasks.

How is the Teacher's Book organised?

Main topics and grammar

Cambridge English: Starters topics and grammar focused on in the activities in this unit.

Story summary

Main vocabulary

Cambridge English: Starters vocabulary focused on in the activities in this unit.

Practice for Starters

Specific activities that gently build up learners' familiarity with the Cambridge English: Starters test task types.

Equipment

Any equipment or materials needed for teaching the unit including photocopiables, digital flashcards, audio.

Let's say!

Optional pronunciation practice for each unit. Storyfun 1 focusses on key sounds for developing early speaking skills in English.

Activity notes

A, B, C etc. sections correspond to Student's Book activities.

Interactive activity

Activity that can also be completed interactively on Presentation Plus.

Answer keys

Answers or suggested answers.

Storytelling

Extended notes for approaching storytelling with your learners give detailed suggestions on how to fully exploit digital resources and prompt meaningful and motivating discussions.

Value

The value can be explored and discussed with learners after reading the story. Discussion is optional, either directly after listening or when learners attempt the value activity.

Extension activities

Flexible ideas to extend activities either in class or for homework.

Test tips and practice

Specific tips for the Cambridge English: Starters test with optional accompanying activity.

Audio

Track listing for accompanying audio on Presentation plus, or online.

Audioscripts

All scripts for listening activities in the Student's Book. Scripts for stories are not listed.

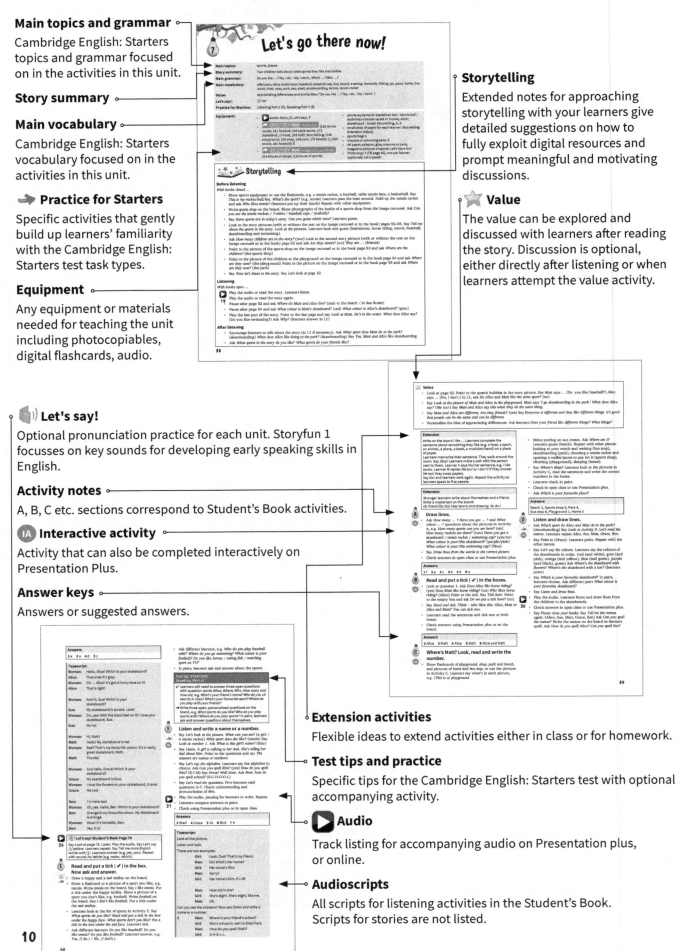

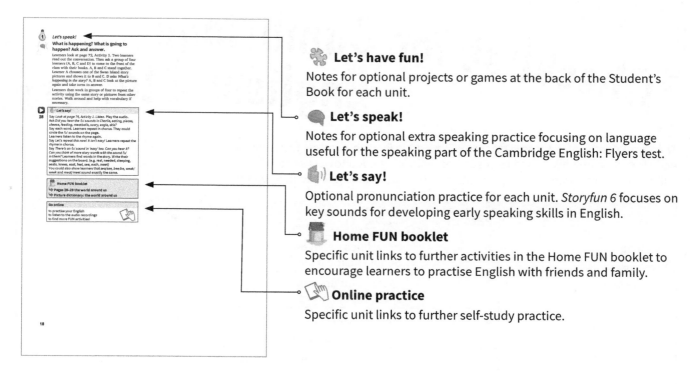

Let's have fun!
Notes for optional projects or games at the back of the Student's Book for each unit.

Let's speak!
Notes for optional extra speaking practice focusing on language useful for the speaking part of the Cambridge English: Flyers test.

Let's say!
Optional pronunciation practice for each unit. *Storyfun 6* focuses on key sounds for developing early speaking skills in English.

Home FUN booklet
Specific unit links to further activities in the Home FUN booklet to encourage learners to practise English with friends and family.

Online practice
Specific unit links to further self-study practice.

How is the digital organised?

Presentation plus

 Interactive activities
Every 'Activity A' in each unit is interactive to check vocabulary comprehension after reading the story and encourage whole-class participation. Other IA activities can be used as a supporting feature, either as a means of introducing an activity, scaffolding, or during answer feedback.

Audio
Audio can be launched from the audio icon.
Accompanying audioscripts can be displayed on screen.

Answer key
All activities have a visual answer key to easily display and check answers with your learners.

Digital flashcards
All Cambridge English: Flyers test words are supported with visual flashcards with accompanying audio.

Image carousel
These additional images can be used to prompt further discussion on themes and concepts. Ideas of when and how to use them are within the teacher's notes for each unit.

Each story also has a collection of separate images of the Student's Book pictures without text to prompt discussion before learners open their books and listen, revise the story if heard in a previous lesson or to use as a wrapping-up activity where learners can re-tell the story they've listened to.

Online practice

For the Teacher
o Presentation plus
o All audio recordings
o Additional digital resources to support your classes

For the Student
o Fun activities to practise the exam, skills and language
o All audio recordings
o Additional digital resources

Word FUN World app

Checklist for Cambridge English: Starters

Storyfun 1 gently introduces learners to Cambridge English: Starters test-style practice. Activities are carefully graded to ensure learners are guided towards the Starters level. Full examples of Cambridge English: Starters test tasks can be found in *Storyfun 2*.

Paper	Part	Task	Unit
Listening 20 minutes 20 questions	1	Draw lines between names and people inside a picture.	Practice: 4, 8
	2	Write numbers and spellings of names.	Practice: 1, 7
	3	Multiple choice. Tick the correct picture.	Practice: 1
	4	Follow instructions and colour parts of a picture.	Practice: 2, 3, 5, 6
Reading and Writing 20 minutes 25 questions	1	Put a tick or cross to show whether the sentence is correct or not for a picture.	Practice: 2
	2	Write *yes* or *no* to show whether a sentence about a picture is true or false.	Practice: 2, 3, 8
	3	Write words, using given jumbled letters, next to a picture.	Practice: 5, 6
	4	Gap fill about an illustrated subject. Write one noun in each gap.	Practice: 8
	5	Write one-word answers to questions about three scene pictures.	Practice: 6
Speaking 3–5 minutes	1	Point to parts of the picture and place object cards in the correct place.	Practice: 1, 4, 6
	2	Answer questions about the picture.	Practice: 2, 3 (*Let's speak!*), 5 (*Let's speak!*),
	3	Answer questions about the remaining object cards.	Practice: 7
	4	Answer personal questions.	Practice: 4, 5, 7 (*Let's speak!*)

Map of the Student's Book

Story and Unit	Value (key phrase)	Topics	Grammar	Practice for Starters
1 Counting	Encouraging others ("*Well done!*")	numbers 1–10 greetings introductions	*My name's / I'm … What's your name? How many …?*	Listening Parts 2 and 3 Speaking Part 1
2 Come and play	Making friends ("*Come and play!*")	toys names pets colours	personal pronouns regular plurals *have got* (for possessions) imperatives question words (*How many?*)	Reading and Writing Parts 1 and 2 Listening Part 4 Speaking Part 2
3 Kim's birthday	Gratitude ("*Thank you!*")	family food colours numbers 6–10	possessive *'s Let's* question words (*How old? How many? Where?*)	Reading and Writing Part 2 Listening Part 4
4 Hugo's school bag	Sharing ("*Here you are!*")	school	*Where's …? Here's my/his/her … What's this?*	Listening Part 1 Speaking Parts 1 and 4
5 What am I?	Asking questions is good ("*Please tell me …*")	animals body and face colours	determiners (*a/an*) *can* (ability) short answers	Reading and Writing Part 3 Listening Part 4 Speaking Part 4
6 Grandma's glasses	Helping others ("*I can help!*")	home family clothes colours	prepositions of place	Reading and Writing Parts 3 and 5 Listening Part 4 Speaking Part 1
7 Let's go there now!	Appreciating differences and similarities ("*Do you like …? Yes, I do. / No, I don't.*")	sports places time	*Do you like …? Yes, I do. / No, I don't. Which …? Who …?*	Listening Part 2 Speaking Part 3
8 Not today!	Apologising ("*Sorry!*")	food animals clothes	*and, but, or Can I/we have …? Yes, you can. / No, you can't. What's this? What are these?*	Reading and Writing Parts 2 and 4 Listening Part 1

Counting

Main topics:	numbers 1–10, (greetings and introductions)
Story summary:	A boy tries to find pairs of shoes in his room, with a little help from his dog.
Main grammar:	*My name's / I'm …*, *What's your name?*, *How many …?*
Main vocabulary:	*bird, black, blue, boots, boy, bye, cat, count, Dan, dog, Eva, fish, friend, girl, good, goodbye, great, he, hello, hi, phone, please, red, right, she, shoe, silly, wave*
Value:	Encouraging others (*"Well done!"*)
Let's say!:	/s/ /ʃ/
Practice for Starters:	Speaking Part 1 (D), Listening Part 2 (E), Listening Part 3 (G)

Equipment:	
• ▶ audio: Story, D, E, Let's say!, G • (presentation **PLUS**) flashcards (59–69 colours, 8 *dog*, 52 *shoes*): Storytelling, A Extension; (74 *girl*, 8 *dog*, 71 *boy*, 138 *phone*): H • (presentation **PLUS**) Image carousel 1–4 (2 pictures of shoes, 2 pictures of boots)	• real pair of boots (optional): Storytelling • ten pieces of A4 paper, each with a number from *one* to *ten* written on it: C Extension • A5 card for each learner: E Extension • Photocopy 1a (TB pages 46–47): E Extension • Photocopy 1b (TB page 48), one per learner: Let's speak! • crayons or colouring pens: C, H, Extension

Storytelling

Before listening

With books closed …

- Say *Hello!* to individual learners. They answer *Hello!* Then say *Hi!* to different learners. They answer *Hi!* Learners practise in pairs.
- Wave to a learner, say *Goodbye!* and turn away. Then say *Bye!* The learner answers *Goodbye!/Bye!* Learners practise in pairs.
- Review/Teach colours, including *red* and *blue*. Point to items in the classroom, or use the flashcards, and ask *What colour is it?*
- Review/Teach *dog* and *shoes* with the flashcards or drawings. Show a real pair of boots. Ask *What colour are my boots?* Show pictures of shoes and boots from the Image carousel. Ask *Are these shoes or boots? What colour are they?*
- Review/Teach numbers *1–10*. Say *Let's count. 1, 2, 3 …*
- Look at the first story picture without the story text on the Image carousel or with the story text in the book on page 4. Say *Tell me about the picture.* Learners say any English words that they can see. Ask *Is the story about a boy or a girl? What animals has he got?* (fish, dog) *Where are his shoes?* (learners point) Learners look at the other story pictures (with or without the text on the Image carousel or in the book) pages 5–7. Say *Tell me about the story.* (Accept suggestions in English or L1.)
- Say *Now let's listen to the story.* Say *Let's look at page 4.*

Listening

With books open …

▶ Play the audio or read the story. Learners listen.

Play the audio or read the story again.

02

- Pause after page 4, point to the picture and ask *What's the boy's name?* (Ben) *What's the dog's name?* (Sam) Say *He counts his …* (shoes) *He counts 1 …* (2, 3)
- Pause after page 5 and say *Look at Ben's shoes. Now he's got 1, 2, 3 …* (4, 5, 6, 7, 8, 9, 10)
- Play the next part of the story. Pause after page 6 to ask *How many shoes can you see?* (eight) Pause after page 7 to ask *What colour are Ben's boots?* (red) Explain *Silly Sam* in L1. Ben loves Sam. He calls Sam silly because he's doing something naughty but also funny. Play the last part of the story and ask *How many shoes and boots can you see?* (ten) *What does Ben say?* (Goodbye!)

After listening

- Talk about the story (in L1 if necessary). Say *Let's count again.* Learners count from *one* to *ten*. Say *Sam plays with Ben's …* (shoes) Ask *Is Sam a good dog?* Learners might have different opinions – encourage discussion and reasons.

- Point to learners' shoes and ask *What colour are your shoes?*
- Ask (in L1 if necessary) *Have you got any pets? What toys do your pets like?*

Value

- Say *Look at page 7*. Point to the speech bubble in the story picture. Say *Ben says ...* (Well done!)
- Ask, in L1, *Why does Ben say 'Well done!'?* (because Sam is helping) Check understanding of *Well done!* (Well done! means *Good job! Thanks!*)
- Say, in L1, *Ben helps us to count. He says 'That's ...'* (right/great) Explain that these phrases encourage others. Ask *Is Sam happy when Ben says 'Well done!'?* (yes) Say *That's right. He is happy and he helps more.*
- Personalise the idea of encouraging others, in L1. Ask *Who says 'Well done!' to you? When? Do you say 'Well done'? Who to? Why?* (e.g. To a friend when they are playing a sport or trying something new or difficult)

Extension

A confident learner counts backwards from *ten* to *one*.
Say *Well done!* The class claps.
In pairs, learners take turns to count from *ten* to *one*.
Circulate and say *Well done!*

 A **IA**

Draw lines.

- Say *Look at the pictures in Activity A*. Point to the four pictures and ask *What's this? And this?* (learners answer)
- In pairs or small groups, learners say the words.
- Do the example. Say *Draw lines from the words to the correct picture.*
- Check answers in open class or use Presentation plus.

Answers

1 d   **2** c   **3** a   **4** b

Extension: Flashcards 59–69 (colours)

Use the flashcards to revise colours.
Play a colour game. Divide the class into teams. Teams line up.
Show a colour flashcard or say the colour word. Say *Look at something (red)*. The learners at the front of the teams race to find an object of this colour. The first learner to find something red gets a point for their team.
The learners go to the back of their teams. Repeat with a different colour and new learners at the front.

 B

Draw, count and write.

- Write numbers *1* to *10* on the board. Point to each number and say the word. Learners join in. Repeat several times.
- Erase one number. Point to the numbers. Say *Let's count again!* Learners say all the numbers, including the missing one. Erase another number. Point and count in open class. Repeat until there are no numbers on the board. Say *That's really great! Well done!*
- Point to the first pair of shoes in Activity B and say *Look! Two shoes.* Ask *What colour are they?* (grey and yellow) Point to the next space and say *Draw and colour this shoe!* Learners draw and colour the missing shoe. Ask *What colour is it?* (black) Point to the two other spaces and say *Now draw these shoes.* Learners draw and colour the missing shoes. Check the colours.
- Point to the first shoe that learners drew. Ask *What number is it? One, two ...* (three) Say *Now you. Count and write.* Learners write the two other numbers.
- Check answers in open class or use Presentation plus.

Answers

black shoe 3   blue shoe 7   red shoe 9

Extension

Show the counting rhyme below on this page on Presentation plus or write it on the board. Say it in open class, holding up fingers as you count:
1, 2, 3,
Count with me!
My name's Ben and I'm your friend.

4, 5, 6,
7 and 8,
That's really, really, really great!

Oh, and then,
It's 9 and 10!
Let's count again!

Learners repeat the rhyme in groups.
Groups say the rhyme for the class.

Test tip: STARTERS
Reading and Writing (Parts 2, 4 and 5), Listening (Parts 2 and 3)

- ✔ Learners should be able to understand numbers *1–20* and their written forms. Some answers in Listening Part 2 will be numbers, but learners write the figures, not the words.
- → Write on the board numbers *1* to *10*, and the number words *one* to *ten* in a different order. Learners take turns to match a figure with a number word.

Extension: ten pieces of A4 paper, each with a number between *one* and *ten* on it

Play a game. Four learners demonstrate. Give one learner one piece of paper with a number word on it. The learner looks, reads and gives you back the paper.
The learner makes a group with the number of learners on their paper.
Ask the class *How many children are here?* Check the answer matches the number.

 C

Read, draw and write.

- Look at the pictures. Ask *Where's the boy? And the girl?* Say *Point to the boy. Point to the girl.* Learners point in their books. Point to learners and say **He's a boy** or **She's a girl.**
- Say the name of a learner. Ask *Boy or girl?* The class say *He's a boy* or *She's a girl.* Repeat.
- Learners read the speech bubbles.

- Point to Eva and ask *What's her name?* Repeat for Dan.
- Point and say *This is you. Draw you and write.* Learners draw themselves and write their names.

> **Extension**
>
> Play a game to practise *Hello* and *Goodbye*.
> Learners stand up. Wave to teach *wave*. Smile, wave and say *Hello*. Learners copy. Turn around and say *Goodbye*. Learners copy and say *Goodbye*.
> Say *Listen and do*. Say *Hello* or *Goodbye*. Learners face you and wave when they hear *Hello* but turn with their backs to you when you say *Goodbye*. They can also play the game in groups or pairs.

D Listen. Ask and answer.

- Point to the speech bubbles. Say *Listen and look*. Play the audio.
- Point to the green speech bubble. Say *Now you!* (Learners say *We're Ben's friends!*).
- Ask different learners *What's your name?* (My name's …)
- Practise in open class.
- Learners stand up and walk around. Say *Stop!* Learners ask and answer *What's your name?* You could play music as they walk.

03

> **Tapescript:**
>
> | Eva and Ben: | We're Ben's friends! |
> |---|---|
> | Eva: | He's a boy. |
> | Dan: | She's a girl. |
> | | What's your name? |

> **Test tip: STARTERS**
> *Speaking (Parts 1 and 4)*
>
> ✔ Learners need to say *Hello* to the examiner and say their name.
> → Encourage learners to say *Hello* at the start of the class and *Goodbye* at the end, as well *Pardon? Sorry? I don't understand* if they want you to repeat a question or instruction.

E Listen and write numbers.

- Look at the picture and ask *What's this?* (a phone) Say *Yes – it's Ben's phone*. Point to the number pad and ask *What's on Ben's phone? Letters or numbers?* (numbers) Ask *What number can you see?* (one) Say *Ben is phoning Eva. What's the phone number?*
- Say *Listen and write numbers*.
- Play the audio. Learners listen and write the phone number. Play the audio again.

04

- Check answers in open class or use Presentation plus.

> **Answer**
>
> 12733658

> **Tapescript:**
>
> | Ben: | Hmm … Oh dear! What's the number? |
> |---|---|
> | | Right. It's 1, 2, 7, 3, 3, 6, 5, 8! |
> | | That's great! |
> | | It's 1, 2, 7, 3, 3, 6, 5, 8. |
> | | … |

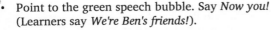

> | Eva: | Hi! |
> |---|---|
> | Ben: | Hi! It's Ben! Hi, Eva! |
> | Eva: | Ha ha! Hi, Ben! |

> **Extension: A5 card for each learner**
>
> Give a piece of A5 card to each learner. They draw a 3 x 4 grid, large enough to write numbers in each square. Say *Let's make a phone. Write the numbers*. They draw the keypad on their card:
>
> | 1 | 2 | 3 |
> |---|---|---|
> | 4 | 5 | 6 |
> | 7 | 8 | 9 |
> | ★ | 0 | # |
>
> Learners work in pairs. Learner A asks *What's your phone number?* Learner B says a phone number. Learner A writes the number and dials it on his/her 'phone'. Learner B watches and makes a ringer noise if it is the right number. Swap roles and repeat.

> **Extension: Photocopiable 1a**
>
> Give each learner a photocopy of '1a Counting' (TB pages 46–47).
> Point to Activity 1 and look at the example. Learners colour numbers *2* to *10*. The circles they choose must touch each other. They compare answers in pairs.
> Ask questions about the pictures in Activity 2, e.g. *Where are the phones? Where are the dogs?* Learners point. Ask *How many shoes can you see?* (five) Show learners the example line from the shoes to the word *five*. Point to the example number *5*. Say *Now you! Count and draw lines. Write the numbers*. Learners work on their own or in pairs to count the items, draw lines to the correct number words and write the numbers. Circulate and ask different learners to count aloud. Check answers in open class.

F Draw lines and say.

- Remind learners of the value discussion when they first read the story (see page 15) or discuss the value now for the first time.
- Look at the pictures. Ask *What's the boy's name?* (Ben) *What's the dog's name?* (Sam) *What colour is the ball?* (red)
- Learners read the speech bubbles. Do number 1 as an example. Say *Draw lines*.
- Learners draw lines from the speech bubbles to the right pictures.
- Check answers and say *Well done!*
- Remind learners that *Well done!* means *Good job! Great!* and practise pronunciation.
- Encourage learners to do actions as they say each phrase (looking down and frowning for *Silly Sam*, patting a dog for *Well done, Sam* and waving and turning around for *Goodbye*).

> **Answers**
>
> 1 c   2 b   3 a

26

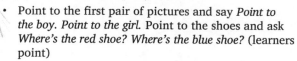

Let's say! **Student's Book Page 74**

Say Look at page 74. *Listen.* Play the audio. Say *Let's say /s/ sun.* Learners repeat. Say *Tell me more English words with /s/.* Learners answer (e.g. six, silly). Repeat with sound /ʃ/ *sh*ell (e.g. she, shoe).

Listen and tick (✔) the box.

- Point to the first pair of pictures and say *Point to the boy. Point to the girl.* Point to the shoes and ask *Where's the red shoe? Where's the blue shoe?* (learners point)
- Ask *Which is correct? Listen and tick the box.* Draw a large tick on the board.

Play the audio.

- Learners listen and tick. Play the audio again.
- Check answers in open class or use Presentation plus.

Answers
Learners tick the following pictures: **2** red shoe   **3** two dogs

Tapescript:		
1	**Boy:**	Hi! Look! There's my friend.
	Man:	Oh! The boy?
	Boy:	Yes!
	Man:	What's the boy's name?
	Boy:	Ben!
2	**Girl:**	Oh! Look! There's my shoe!
	Boy:	The red shoe?
	Girl:	Yes! It's a red shoe.
	Sam:	Woof!
3	**Man:**	Oh! Look! Two dogs!
	Girl:	Wow!
	Man:	Two dogs!
	Girl:	Cool!

Read and draw.

- Review/Teach some common classroom object words, e.g. *books, pencils, pens, bags.* Practise *How many …?* Ask *How many* questions (with answers between *one* and *ten*), pointing to windows, books and pens.
- Draw a large box on the board and write *Four shoes* under it. Draw four shoes in the box. Say *Let's count the shoes.* Count them. Ask *How many?* (four) Practise the words from Activity H (*girl, dog, boy, phone*) with the flashcards or pictures from the story.
- Point to the four boxes in the book and say *Read and draw.* Learners read the words and draw items in each box.
- Learners compare their pictures in pairs. They encourage each other with *Well done!*

Answers
Learners draw one girl, one dog, two boys and three phones.

Extension
Learners draw four empty boxes on a piece of paper. Above each box they write a question, e.g. *How many cats?* and they write the answer below the box, e.g. *Six cats.* Then they swap papers, read and draw.

Let's have fun!

Count and tick (✔). How many?

Say *Ben counts his shoes in the story. What things can you count?*

Ask different learners to point to something red / something blue. Say *Look! That's red!* or *Look! That's blue!*

Learners work in pairs. They point to things in the classroom that are red or blue and say *Look! That's red!* or *Look! That's blue!*

Learners look at SB page 68 Activity 1. Say *Let's have fun! Let's count and tick!*

Learners add ticks to their table for each item.

Learners count the number of ticks and write the totals in the last boxes.

Ask different learners *How many red/blue things can you see?*

Ask stronger learners to name their red or blue objects.

Say *Ben counts his shoes in the story. What things do you count at home?* Prompt if necessary. Ask, e.g. *Do you count your pencils/crayons/games/books/ toys/T-shirts?*

Let's speak!

How many …? Play a game.

Ask learners to turn to page 72 in their Student's Book and look at Activity 1.

Give each learner a photocopy of '1b How many?' (TB page 48). Point to the first box and say *Look at the dogs.* Ask *How many dogs can you see?* (two) Ask *Where are the girls?* (learners point) Ask *How many girls can you see?* (three)

In L1, ask learners to cut the paper to make pairs of cards. Make sure the cards are mixed up. Each group places their cards face down. Learners take it in turns to turn over two cards and say how many they can see, e.g. *one (frog), two (dogs).* If the cards aren't a matching pair, they replace the cards face down. If the cards do match, learners say, e.g. *Two and two. Yes!* and keep the pair. The next learner then turns over two cards. The game ends when all the cards are matched.

Learners say *Well done!* to congratulate each other.

Home FUN booklet
➡ **Pages 4–5 numbers**
➡ **Picture dictionary: animals, colours**

Go online
to practise your English to listen to the audio recordings to find more FUN activities!

Come and play

Main topics:	toys, animals
Story summary:	Four children talk about their toys and pets and invite the reader to join in with their games.
Main grammar:	personal pronouns (*I, you, we, me, my*), regular plurals, *have got*
Main vocabulary:	*Anna, bag, ball, bat, big, bike, book, car, children, doll, duck, frog, funny, green, guitar, hand, hat, kite, lizard, mouse, Pat, pear, pencil, pet, robot, Sue, teddy bear, Tom, truck, yellow*
Value:	Making friends ("*Come and play!*")
Let's say!:	/ɪ/ /æ/ /e/
Practice for Starters:	Reading and Writing Part 1 (C), Speaking Part 2 (E), Reading and Writing Part 2 (F), Listening Part 4 (F)

Equipment:	
• ▶ audio: Story, F, Let's say! • ➔ presentation **PLUS** flashcards (210 *teddy bear*, 182 *guitar*, 203 *ball*, 176 *bike*, 186 *kite*, 215 *truck*, 207 *doll*, 209 *robot*, 213 *car*, 8 *dog*, 4 *cat*, 10 *duck*, 13 *frog*, 19 *lizard*): Storytelling • ➔ presentation **PLUS** Image carousel 5–10 (3 pictures of toys, 3 pictures of animals): D Extension	• real guitar and toys from the story (e.g. bat, truck, doll, teddy bear, car): Storytelling, Storytelling Extension • Photocopy 2 (TB page 49), one per group of three or four learners: Let's speak! • crayons or colouring pens: G, Let's have fun! • A4 paper or card for each learner: C, Let's have fun! • old magazines (optional): Let's have fun! • soft ball: H Extension • hat: Let's speak!

 ## Storytelling

Before listening

With books closed …

- Ask *Have you got a book?* (show a book) *A bike?* (mime cycling) *Have you got a guitar?* (mime playing a guitar) *What have you got?* Learners say and mime toys. Review/Teach *teddy bear, guitar, ball, bike, kite, truck, doll, robot* and *car* with the flashcards.
- Ask *What animals have you got? Have you got a cat?* Miaow. *Have you got a dog?* Bark. Say *Pets are animals at home.* Explain in L1 if necessary. Use the flashcards or drawings to revise *dog, cat, duck, frog* and *lizard.*
- Look at the first story picture without the story text on the Image carousel or with the story text in the SB page 12. Ask *What can you see?* (A girl. Two cars. Four guitars.)
- Look at all the story pictures (with or without the text on the Image carousel or in the book) pages 12–15. Ask *How many children can you see?* (four) *How many girls?* (two) *How many boys?* (two)
- Say *Now let's listen to the story.* Say *Let's look at page 12.*

Listening

With books open …

Play the audio or read the story. Learners listen.

06 Play the audio or read the story again.

Pause after page 12 and ask *What's the girl's name?* (Anna) Point and ask *What's this?* (a car / a guitar / a kite / a bike)

- Pause after page 13 and ask about Tom. Repeat for Sue and Pat on page 14.

After listening

- Talk about the story (in L1 if necessary). Ask *What toys do you like? What animals do you like?* Point to the children in the pictures. Say *This is …* (Anna) *Anna likes …* (the guitar)

 ### Value

- Look at the speech bubble on page 12. Ask *What does Anna say? Come and …* (play with me today!) Check understanding of *Come and play.*
- Look at page 14. In L1 (if necessary), ask *Who is this?* (Sue) *And who is this?* (Pat) Say *Sue and Pat are friends. What do they say? Come and …* (play with us today!)
- Ask, in L1, *Why do Sue and Pat say 'Come and play'?* (they want to make friends)
- Personalise the idea of making friends, in L1. Ask *How do you make friends? Which games do you like playing with your friends?*

A Draw lines.

- Learners look at the pictures. Say *Look! What is this toy?* (a kite) *What are these animals?* (a duck, a frog) *What is this fruit?* (a pear)

- Do number 1 as an example. Say *Now you! Draw lines.*

- Check answers in open class or use Presentation plus.

Answers

1 b   **2** a   **3** c   **4** d

B Look, read and write the names.

- Remind learners of the value discussion when they first read the story (see page 18) or discuss the value now for the first time.

- Ask three or four learners *What's your name?* (learners answer)

- Point to the same learners and ask others *What's his/ her name?* Say *His name's ...* (learner's name) and *Her name's ...* (learner's name)

- Point to the picture of Anna. Ask *What's her name?* (Anna)

- Say *Write the friends' names.* Learners look at the pictures and write the names on the dotted lines.

Answers

Left to right: Anna, Tom, Sue, Pat

C Put a tick (✔) or a cross (✖) in the box.

- Look at the examples. Point to the bike and ask *Is this a bike?* (yes) Draw a big tick in the air. Say *Yes. This is a bike.* Point to the bat and ask *Is this a duck?* (no) Draw a big cross in the air. Say *No. This is a ...* (bat)

- Learners look, read and put a tick or a cross. They check answers in pairs.

- Ask what they can see in pictures 2, 4, 5 and 8. Stronger learners can write sentences: 1 *This is a bike.* 2 *This is a bat*, etc.

Answers

3 ✔   **4** ✖   **5** ✖   **6** ✔   **7** ✔   **8** ✖

D Look and write.

- Hold up one book and say *I've got a book. I've got one book.* Write on the board: *I've got a book. = I've got one book.*

- Hold up two books and say *I've got two books.* Write on the board: *I've got two book ...* (s) Point to the end of the word and ask *Book or books?* (books) Emphasise the 's' sound. Learners draw an 's' shape in the air. Repeat with three pencils and four pens.

- Point to Activity D and do the example. Say *Look and write.* Learners look at the picture and write the missing words on the lines.

Answers

2 bike   **3** guitar   **4** duck   **5** hats   **6** kites   **7** bats
8 dolls   **9** pencils   **10** books

E Look and say.

- Say *Look at the pictures.* Point to the robot and say *Here's the robot. Now listen and point. Where's the dog/ cat/mouse? Where are the ducks/books/kites?*

- Review/Teach *I've/She's/He's/They've got.* Hold up six pencils and say *I've got six pencils.* Ask a learner *How many pencils have you got?* (I've got three pencils.) Ask another learner *How many pencils has she/he got?* (She's/He's got three pencils.) Ask a pair about another pair *How many books have they got?* (They've got four books.)

- In groups of four, learners look at Activity E. One pair looks at the first picture and the other pair looks at the second picture.

- Pairs take turns to say something about their picture, e.g. *They've got four hats. They've got seven kites.*

F. Look and read. Write *yes* or *no*.

- Point to Pat/Tom. Ask *What's his name?* (Pat/Tom)
  Point to Sue/Anna. Ask *What's her name?* (Sue/Anna)
  Point to the big robot and ask *What colour are his pencils?* (red, yellow, blue, green)
- Do the examples. In pairs, learners read the other sentences and write *yes* or *no*.

Answers
3 yes **4** no **5** yes **6** no **7** no

Test tip: STARTERS *Reading and Writing (Part 2)*
✔ The picture sentences are sometimes about colour or number, e.g. *The books are red. There are two books.* → Write sentences on the board about a picture, e.g. *Sue has got a guitar. Tom's hat is yellow.* Learners look at the picture and write *yes* or *no*.

Listen and colour.

- Check each learner has red, yellow, blue and green pencils.
- Review/Teach *on*. For example, put a toy frog/spider on your hand, look scared and say *Oh no! Look! A frog is on my hand!* Say *Point to the robot ... with the pencils. / on the cat. / on the book. / on the table.*
- Say *Listen and colour the robots.* In L1, tell learners they can colour the tops of the robots' heads first. They can finish colouring at the end of the activity.

07

- Play the audio. Pause the recording after the first colouring instruction and say *One robot has got some pencils. What colour is that robot now?* (green) Say *Now you! Listen and colour.* Play the rest of the audio. Learners check their colouring. Ask questions: *What colour is the robot on the book now?* (red) *And what colour is the robot on the cat?* (blue)
- Check answers.

Answers
the robot on the book – red the robot on the table – yellow the robot on the cat – blue

Tapescript:		
1	**Woman:**	Look! One robot has got some pencils.
	Boy:	That's right ... It's funny!
	Woman:	Colour that robot green.
	Boy:	Sorry? Colour it green?
	Woman:	Yes, please.
2	**Woman:**	And look! There's a robot on a book.
	Boy:	Oh, yes! A robot is on the book.
	Woman:	Colour it red.
	Boy:	Colour it with my red pencil?
	Woman:	Yes. That's right.

3	**Boy:**	And one robot's on the table. Look!
	Woman:	Yes! Colour it yellow.
	Boy:	Colour the robot on the table yellow?
	Woman:	Yes.
	Boy:	OK.
4	**Boy:**	The cat has got a small toy robot, too. Look!
	Woman:	Yes, the cat has got a robot, too. Colour it blue.
	Boy:	Pardon? Colour it blue?
	Woman:	Yes, please.
	Boy:	There.
	Woman:	Well done!

G. Write and draw.

- Look at the example sentence and picture in the book.
- Point to picture 2 and ask *What's this?* (a cat) Say *Write 'cat' and then draw the cat.* Learners complete the sentence and join the dots to complete the cat.
- Revise and write on the board *kite, bat, hat, duck, truck, doll, pear, lizard.* Learners choose three and draw them in the boxes.
- In pairs, Learner A completes Learner B's sentences, and Learner B completes Learner A's sentences. They swap books again and check answers. Encourage learners to look at each other's pictures and say *That's great! Well done!*

H Say the words. Draw lines.

- Point to each star. Ask *What colour is this? And this? And this?* (blue/red/yellow)
- Point to the words and ask *What's the blue/red/yellow word?* (truck/frog/Pat) Repeat the words in open class.
- Say *Now look at the words in the box.*
- Ask, in L1 if necessary, *Which words sound the same?* Point to *Pat* and say *Pat and …* (cat, hat) Learners draw lines from *bat, cat* and *hat* to the yellow star.
- Repeat with *truck* and *frog*.

Answers
pat: cat, hat   truck: duck   frog: dog

▶ 26 ◀)) *Let's say! Student's Book Page 74*

Say *Look at page 74. Listen.* Play the audio. Say *Let's say /ɪ/ tennis.* Learners repeat. Say *Tell me more English words with /ɪ/.* Learners answer (e.g. big, lizard). Repeat with sound /æ/ *hand* (e.g. bag, hat) and /e/ *bed* (e.g. pet, teddy).

2 Let's have fun!

Make a poster.

Say *Tom has got some red hats. I've got a yellow hat.* Draw a picture of a yellow hat and write on the board: *I've got a yellow hat.*

Learners say more colour words they know (green, blue). Review/Teach more colour words, e.g. *white* and *black.*

Learners look at SB page 68 Activity 2. Say *Let's have fun! Let's make a poster!*

Learners look in magazines and find four things or draw and colour four things on a sheet of paper, e.g. a bike, a skateboard, a cat, a teddy bear. They write *I've got …* (e.g. a bike).

Display the posters if possible.

2 Let's speak!

Come and play with me today!
Ask and answer.

Make cards with the photocopy of '2 Come and play with me today!' (TB page 49).

Put an even number of lizard (*L*), cat (*C*), robot (*R*) and duck (*D*) cards folded in a hat. Move desks to make space or play the game in the playground.

Say *In this game, lizards find lizards, cats find cats, robots find robots and ducks find ducks!*

Two learners demonstrate with you. They each take a card out of the hat and look at their letter. You also take out a card (e.g. *D*). Say *I'm a duck! Where's a duck?*

Teacher:	Are you a duck?
Learner A:	No!
Teacher:	Are you a duck?
Learner B:	Yes!
Teacher:	Come and play with me today!

Each learner takes a folded card from the hat but keeps it secret.

Learners walk around and play the game.

 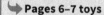

Home FUN booklet
➡ Pages 6–7 toys
➡ Picture dictionary: animals, toys, colours

Go online
to practise your English to listen to the audio recordings to find more FUN activities!

Kim's birthday

3

Main topics:	family
Story summary:	It's Kim's birthday and she has a party at home with her family, with presents, balloons and cake.
Main grammar:	*This is my …, These are my …, Is this …? No, it's / they're …,* Question words (*How old? How many? Where?*)
Main vocabulary:	*balloon, Bill, birthday, brother, cake, clock, dad, Dan, fun, get, grandma, grandpa, hat, hooray, ice cream, Jill, lemonade, make, mum, new, paint, sing, sister, sock, song, spider, thank you, tiger, toy, wow!*
Value:	Gratitude (*"Thank you!"*)
Let's say!:	/p/ /b/ /d/ /t/
Practice for Starters:	Reading and Writing Part 2 (E), Listening Part 4 (F)
Equipment:	• ▶ audio: Story, F, I, Let's say! • ➡ presentation **PLUS** flashcards (199 *birthday party*, 93 *ice cream*, 84 *cake*, 97 *lemonade*): Storytelling; (78 *mum*, 74 *dad*, 79 *sister*, 76 *grandma*): B; (27 *tiger*): C; (203–219 *toys*): H • wrapped box to look like present, birthday card, two or three balloons (optional): Storytelling, A • ➡ presentation **PLUS** Image carousel 11–18 (3 pictures of families, 1 picture of paints, 4 pictures of birthday cards)(optional): B • large soft bag and six to eight known objects, e.g. toy car, ball, toy boat, doll, card (optional): C Extension • crayons or colouring pens: F, H • box of paints or picture of paints from Image carousel (optional): F • real birthday cards with ages (or pictures from the Image carousel), sheets of paper or card, materials for decorating birthday cards, e.g. glitter, glue, stickers: Project

 Storytelling

Before listening

With books closed …

- You can decorate the classroom with balloons. Point to the balloons and teach *balloons*. Show a flashcard or picture of a birthday party and teach *birthday party*. In L1, teach *birthday* by asking different learners when their birthday is. Show a wrapped present and ask *What's this?* Teach *present*.
- Ask *What party food do you like?* Review/Teach *ice cream, cake* and *lemonade* with flashcards or pictures.
- Look at the pictures of the present and the party without the story text on the Image carousel or with the story text in the book on page 20. Say *This story is about 'Kim's birthday'.* Say *Look at the picture.* Ask *Is Kim a boy or a girl?* (learners guess – girl) Ask *Where is Kim?* Learners guess and point to the picture.
- Learners look at the other story pictures (with or without the text on the Image carousel or in the book) pages 21–23. Ask *How many presents can you see? What presents can you see?*
- Say *Now let's listen to the story.* Say *Let's look at page 20.*

Listening

With books open …

 Play the audio or read the story. Learners listen.
Play the audio or read the story again.

08
- Pause after the first section and ask *What are their names? Kim's brother is …* (Dan) *Kim's sister is …* (Jill) *Kim's grandpa is …* (Bill)
- Pause halfway through page 21 and say *Bill says 'Let's make a big …'* (cake!)
- Pause halfway through page 22 and ask *How many presents has Kim got?* (three) Point and say *Kim's got a hat, some socks and a …* (toy spider)
- Pause after page 22 and ask *Where's the toy spider?* (on Grandpa's head)
- At the end of the story ask *What does Kim say?* (Thank you!)

After listening

- Talk about the story. Ask *How old is Kim?* (eight) *How many people are at the party?* (six) *What do they do at the party?* (sing, eat cake, have fun)
- In L1, ask about Kim's presents, e.g. *What present do you like? What present is funny?*

A

Draw lines.

- Learners look at the pictures. They repeat the four words.
- In pairs, learners say the words. Say *Draw lines from the pictures to the correct word.*
- Check answers in open class or use Presentation plus.

Answers

1 c   2 b   3 d   4 a

 B

Look, read and write.

- Show pictures of a family from the Image carousel or use flashcards. Point and say, e.g. *This is Grace. This is her ...* (mum) *This is her ...* (dad) *This is her ...* (sister) *This is her ...* (grandma)
- Look at Activity B. One learner reads Kim's speech bubble. Do the example.
- Point to the pictures and say *Now look at these pictures. Write the family words.*
- Learners complete the sentences. They can check the story to help.
- Check answers in open class or use Presentation plus.

Answers

2 brother   3 dad   4 sister   5 grandpa

Extension

Learners draw the faces of their family and write, e.g. *My mum, My brother.*

 C

Which are Kim's presents? Put a tick (✔) or a cross (✘) in the box.

- Look at the pictures and say *Where's the hat/bat/clock?* Learners point. Review/Teach *tiger* with a flashcard or picture. Show a sock. Say *This is a ...* (sock)
- Point to the clock. Ask *Is this one of Kim's presents?* (no) Say *Put a cross in that box.*
- Say *Now you! Put a tick or a cross.*
- Check answers in open class.

Answers

1 ✘   2 ✘   3 ✔   4 ✘   5 ✔   6 ✔

 D

Read and choose a word. Write.

- Explain, in L1 if necessary, that we use *Let's* to suggest what to do.
- Point to the pictures in Activity D (or on Presentation plus) and say *Let's look at the words and pictures.* Learners look at the six pictures and the words in the box.
- Do the example.
- Learners complete the speech bubbles.
- Check answers in open class.

Answers

2 hats   3 cake   4 songs   5 balloons   6 lemonade

- Play a game to practise the language. Do an action, e.g. stirring cake mixture. Say *Let's make a ...* (cake) Repeat for *sing a ...* (song), *get some ...* (balloons), and *have some ...* (lemonade).

Test tip: STARTERS
Reading and Writing (Part 4)

✔ When learners have to write missing words, it will help them choose a singular or plural answer if they look carefully at the words before the gap.

→ Write on the board *a, lots of / some*. With learners' help, add four words from the story, e.g. *a cake/balloon/hat/sock; lots of / some cakes/balloons/hats/socks.* Say *Find some balloons in Activity D.* Learners point.

Extension

Make a happy face and say *I'm happy*. Make a sad face and say *Now I'm sad.*
On the board, draw a happy and sad smiley (☺☹). Write *OK! Great!* and *No! Not now!* Practise the two phrases with expression.
Make suggestions with *Let's ...* and learners answer, e.g. *Let's play a game!* (OK! Great!) *Let's write lots of long words!* (No! Not now!) *Let's eat some cake!* (OK! Great!)

 E

Look and read. Write *yes* or *no*.

- Learners look at the picture. Ask *How many people can you see?* (three) *They are ...* (Kim, Grandpa Bill, Jill) *Can you see a clock?* (yes) *How many balloons are there?* (five) *Can you see the toy tiger?* (no)
- Do the examples. In pairs, learners read the other sentences and write *yes* or *no*.

Answers

3 no   4 yes   5 yes   6 no

- Stronger learners can write correct versions of sentences 2, 3 and 6.

Test tip: STARTERS
Reading and Writing (Part 2)

✔ In Reading and Writing Part 2, learners write *yes* or *no* to show if each sentence is right or wrong.
→ Find another picture from this story and show it to the class. On the board, write two correct sentences and two wrong sentences about the picture. In pairs, learners quietly decide if the answer is *yes* or *no*. Point to the sentences in open class. Pairs call out *yes* or *no* in chorus.

Listen and colour.

- Point to the picture in Activity F. Ask *What's this?* (a paintbox) Say *It's Kim's present.* Revise the colours using a box of paints or a picture from the Image carousel. Point to each colour and ask *What colour is this? And this? Is this red? Look! This is …*
- Say *Look at the numbers. Let's count!* Point to the numbers on the paints. Learners count in chorus.
- Check each learner has crayons (including the colours brown, green, pink and purple).
- Say *Listen and colour.*
- Play the audio. Pause after colouring '2'. Ask *What colour is this paint?* (green)

09
- Play the rest of the audio. Play the audio again. Check answers. Call out numbers. Learners call out colours.

Answers
Learners colour the following numbers:
2 green   4 purple   6 pink   8 brown

Tapescript:

Girl:	Wow! A paintbox. Can I colour it?
Man:	Yes, you can. Colour number 2 green.
Girl:	Number 2? Green?
Man:	Yes, please!
Man:	Now colour number 4.
Girl:	Sorry! What colour?
Man:	Colour number 4. Purple! Yes, purple!
Girl:	OK. I love that colour.
Man:	Look! There's number 6. Can you see number 6?
Girl:	Yes! Is that pink?
Man:	Yes. Colour that pink!
Man:	And now number 8.
Girl:	Number 8? Great!
Man:	Colour it brown.
Girl:	OK. It's brown now. Look!
Man:	Hooray!

Test tip: STARTERS
Listening (Part 4)

✔ There are 11 Starter colours: white, black, blue, brown, green, grey, orange, pink, purple, red and yellow.
→ Make sure learners understand the colours. Ask *What colour …?* questions as often as you can in lessons.

Draw lines.

- Write three questions on the left of the board and answers on the right, mixed up, e.g. *How old are you? What's your name? Where's your book? It's on my desk. I'm Maria. I'm ten.* Three learners draw a line to match a question and an answer.
- Look at Activity G and do the example.
- Learners read and draw lines. They can compare answers in pairs.
- Check answers in open class.

Answers
2 d   **3** c   **4** a   **5** b

- Divide learners into two groups. Practise each dialogue for groups to repeat.

Draw your present for Kim.

- Remind learners of the value discussion when they first read the story (see page 23) or discuss the value now for the first time.
- Say *You give Kim a present now. You choose. Draw it in the box.* Learners decide and draw their present in the box. They can choose any present. Circulate and ask *What's your present?* Help with vocabulary if necessary, using toys flashcards.
- Two or three learners show their present and say *This is (a bike).*

Extension
Put learners into new pairs. Give each learner a piece of paper. Say *Draw a present for your friend.* Demonstrate the activity. Draw a toy on a piece of paper and fold it to hide the picture. Draw a wrapped present on the top of the folded paper. Confirm the instructions in L1.
Point to the picture of Kim in Activity H and ask *What does Kim say?* (Thank you!) Write more things Kim could say on the board, e.g. *It's a toy spider! Wow! It's really great!* Practise the phrases with the class.
Give the present you drew to a learner and say *Happy birthday! Here you are! Open it now!*
The learner opens the present and says *What is it? Thank you!*
Ask *Do you like it?* If the learner answers *Yes*, say *Great!* If they answer *No*, say *Oh! Sorry!*
Learners exchange their presents in pairs. They say *Happy birthday!* and *Thank you!*
Repeat with new partners.

Listen and sing the song.

- Learners work in groups of four. Ask story questions. Groups quickly discuss and write answers. Questions: *1 Kim is with her …* (mum, dad, brother, sister and grandpa) *2 What's Kim's sister's name?* (Jill) *3 How old is Kim today?* (eight) *4 What presents has she got?* (a box of paints, a sun hat, some socks, a toy spider) *5 What do they eat at the party?* (cake) *6 What do they drink?* (lemonade)

- Say *Kim is very happy. She sings a song. Let's look at the words*. Read the first verse of the song line by line. Stop at the missing words and ask *What's the word?* Learners guess (they don't write yet). Read the second verse. Encourage the class to join in and read it with you.

10
- Say *Listen and write the missing words*. Play the first verse of the song. Pause for learners to write the words. They compare their answers in pairs. Check answers.

- Play the song again.

Answers
1 Dad   **2** cake   **3** eight

Tapescript:
See TB page 57

- Play the audio again. Learners sing as they listen.
- Say *Now stand up*. Teach learners actions for the words as follows:

    It's my birthday today! Hooray! Hooray! – clap your hands

    It's a happy, happy, happy, happy day. – jump up and down

    Mum and Dad are here. And Jill! – point to another part of the room

    My brother Dan and Grandpa Bill. – wave

    We've got lemonade – mime drinking

    and chocolate cake. – mime eating a piece of cake

    And now I'm not seven. Now I'm eight! – hold up eight fingers

    Thank you, Mum and Dad and Jill.

    And thank you, Dan and Grandpa Bill. – stretch out arms and smile

- Play the song. Learners do the actions.
- You can also listen to a version of this song without the words for learners to sing along to.

27

26
🔊)) *Let's Say!* **Student's Book Page 74**
Say *Look at page 74. Listen*. Play the audio. Say *Let's say /p/ **p**iano*. Learners repeat. Say *Tell me more English words with /p/*. Learners answer (e.g. paint, pencil). Repeat with sounds /b/ **b**anana (e.g. balloon, birthday), /d/ **d**oll (e.g. dad, Dan) and /t/ **t**eddy bear (e.g. tiger, toy).

3

Let's have fun!
Make a birthday card.

Revise numbers *six* to *ten*. Ask *How old are you?* (learners answer) Write the question on the board. Drill the question and answer chorally. Learners ask and answer the question in closed pairs or walk around the classroom and ask other classmates.

Show real birthday cards with ages on, or pictures of birthday cards from the Image carousel. Ask *How old is he/she?* Learners say the age. Ask *What's in the card?* Show some messages in the real cards and/or write them on the board, e.g. *Happy Birthday!* Explain that we usually write *(Love) from …* in a card, with crosses to represent kisses.

Learners look at SB page 69 Activity 3. Say *Let's have fun! Let's make Kim some birthday cards!* Ask *How old is Kim?* (She's eight.)

Give learners coloured paper or card and materials for decorating (glue, glitter, ribbons, scissors, sticky silver stars, old magazines with pictures). Learners make their cards. They decorate the front and write a greeting and their name inside. They can use the birthday card on SB page 69 as a model.

Display the cards if possible.

3

Let's speak!
What is it? Play a game.

In pairs, learners draw something on a piece of paper. They fold the paper over in three parts or use their hands to hide the picture. Learners ask *What is it?* Their partner guesses *Is it a …?* If the answer is wrong, the learner opens the paper up once or moves their hands a little to show a bit of the picture. Each learner can have three guesses. Learners say *Yes, Well done!* or *No*.

🏠 **Home FUN booklet**
➡ **Pages 8–9 family**
➡ **Picture dictionary: family, food, colours**

Go online
to practise your English to listen to the audio recordings to find more FUN activities!

Hugo's school bag

Main topics:	school
Story summary:	Hugo gets all his things ready for school and catches the bus. He loses his things on the way to school but his friends all share with him so he can make a poster.
Main grammar:	*Where's …?, Here's my/his/her …, What's this?*
Main vocabulary:	*bus, catch, classmates, classroom, cool, crayons, don't worry, eraser, fantastic, Grace, Hugo, jump, lesson, Mark, May, Nick, pen, playground, ruler, run, school, smile, Sue, teacher*
Value:	Sharing - ("*Here you are!*")
Let's say!:	/ʌ/ /ɒ/ /ʊ/
Practice for Starters:	Speaking Part 1 (C), Listening Part 1 (F), Speaking Part 4 (H)

Equipment:

- ▶ audio: Story, D, I, Let's say!
- ↪ (presentation **PLUS** flashcards)

  (42 *bag*, 158 *crayons*, 167 *eraser*, 163 *ruler*, 154 *book*, 164 *pen*, 149 *playground*, 169 *teacher*): Storytelling
- school bag with classroom items inside (optional): Storytelling, A, G

- ↪ (presentation **PLUS** Image carousel 19–22)

  (4 pictures of classrooms) (optional): Storytelling, A, Extension
- blindfold: B Extension
- Photocopy 4a (TB pages 50–51): E Extension
- Photocopy 4b (TB page 52), one per learner: Let's have fun!
- A4 piece of blank paper, one per learner: Let's speak!

 Storytelling

Before listening

With books closed …

- Show photographs of classrooms around the world from the Image carousel. Say *It's a school day today. We're at school.*
- Show a school bag or a flashcard. Ask *What's this?* (bag) Say *It's a bag for school. It's a school bag.* Say *Show me your school bag.* (learners point)
- If you have a bag with objects, say *What's in this bag?* Show learners a book. Ask *What's this?* (a book) Take school items out of the bag. Say, e.g. *This is a ruler. What is it? It's a …* (ruler) Repeat with crayons, an eraser and a pen.
- Revise key vocabulary using the flashcards (*bag, crayons, rubber, eraser, book, pen*).
- Review/Teach *classroom* and *playground*. Show the word *class* in *classroom* and *play* in *playground*. Say *You have lessons in a …* (classroom) *You play in a …* (playground)
- Look at the picture of the breakfast scene without the story text on the Image carousel or with the story text in the book on page 28. Ask *What's the boy's name?* (Hugo) *Is he at school or at home?* (home) *What can you see in the picture?* (a computer, his school bag)
- Learners look at the other story pictures (with or without the text on the Image carousel or in the book) pages 29–31. On page 30 ask *Is this Hugo's sister?* (no) *It's Hugo's …* (teacher)
- Say *Now let's listen to the story.* Say *Let's look at page 28.*

Listening

With books open …

 Play the audio or read the story. Learners listen.

Play the audio or read the story again.

11
- Pause after page 28 and ask *What's in Hugo's school bag?* (crayons, paints, an eraser, a phone, a ruler, a book and a pen)
- Pause after page 29 and ask, in L1 if necessary, *Who's Sue?* (sister) *Who are Grace and Nick?* (friends) Say *Look at Hugo's ruler. Where is it?* (learners point to it falling out of his bag) Say *Oh, no!* Encourage learners to repeat this phrase with feeling.
- Pause after page 30 and say *In the playground Hugo …* (plays/jumps/runs) Ask *What can you see here?* (his pen) Say *Oh, no!* again. Learners join in.
- At the end of the story ask *Has Hugo got his ruler?* (no) *And his pen?* (no) Say *Look! Mark gives Hugo a …* (ruler)

After listening

- In L1 if necessary, encourage learners to talk about the problem with Hugo's school bag.
- Ask *What is in your school bag?*

⭐ **Value**

- Look at page 31. Point to the speech bubbles in the story picture. Say *Mark says ...* (Here you are!) Ask *Who gives Hugo a pen?* (May)
- Give a pencil to a learner and say *Here you are!* Practise pronunciation. Say *Hugo's friends share their things.* Explain the meaning of *share.* Ask *What does Hugo say at the end of the story?* (Thank you!)
- In L1, ask *How does Hugo feel when he can't find his ruler and his pen?* (worried) *Is he worried at the end?* (no)
- Personalise the idea of sharing. Ask *Who do you share with? When do we need to share? Do you know anyone who is good at sharing?*
- With stronger learners, talk about the other phrases Hugo's friends use when they give him their things: *Don't worry! It's OK! Have my ...*

A Draw lines.

- Show learners a book/pencil. Say *Here's my book. And here's my pencil.* Ask a confident learner to stand up and show the class his/her classroom objects. Learners repeat the activity in pairs.
- Learners look at the pictures. Different learners mime giving or pointing and read out the sentences.
- Ask *Where's the picture of a pen? And its sentence?* Learners point. Say *Draw lines!*
- Check answers in open class or use Presentation plus.

Answers					
1 e	2 a	3 c	4 f	5 b	6 d

B Look, read and write.

- Write the story names on the board: *Hugo, Miss Rice, Nick, Mark, Grace, May* and *Sue.* Point to picture 1 and say *This is ...* (Hugo's sister) Learners come to the board, point to and say the correct name (Sue).
- Erase the names from the board. Say *Read the questions and complete the names.*
- Learners work in pairs and write the names. Check answers. Ask different learners *How do you spell that name?* or use Presentation plus.

Answers				
2 Miss Rice	3 Grace	4 Nick	5 Mark	6 May

Test tip: STARTERS
Reading and Writing (all parts), Listening (all parts)

✔ Learners need to understand the following names for the Starters Test: *Alex, Alice, Anna, Ben, Bill, Dan, Eva, Grace, Hugo, Jill, Kim, Lucy, Mark, Matt, May, Nick, Pat, Sam, Sue* and *Tom.*
➜ After working on a story with two or more names, tell learners to close their books. Ask *What's the girl's/boy's name in the story? How do you spell their name?*

Extension

Practise *What's his/her name?* Learner A stands with their back to the class. Say to another learner (learner B) *Say hello to your friend.* Gesture that the class needs to be quiet. Learner B says *Hello!* Learner A tries to recognise Learner B's voice. Ask *What's his/her name?* Learner A has three guesses. When they guess correctly, another learner comes to the front.

C Ask and answer. Look and point.

- Learners look at the picture. Use Presentation plus if possible. Say *Look! It's a school. Where are the children?* (in the playground) Ask *How many teachers are there?* (two) *What colour is the ball?* (brown)
- Ask different learners to come to the front. Ask *Where's / Where are the ...?* See possible questions below. Learners find the item(s) in the picture and point. Revise the difference between *Where's* and *Where are* (they look for one or more things).
- Two learners read out the speech bubbles to the class.
- Learners ask in pairs *Where's / Where are the ...?* The learner points and answers *Here!*
- Possible questions: *Where's the car/football/ skateboard/robot/sun/helicopter/balloon/clock/jacket/ girl? Where are the boys/teachers/birds/trees?*

Test tip: STARTERS
Speaking (Part 1)

✔ In the test, the examiner asks one *Where's the ...?* question and one *Where are the ...?* question about a big picture. Learners listen and point.
➜ Using big pictures in the SB, ask, as often as possible, *Where's / Where are ...?* questions. Learners point and say *Here!*

Extension

Use the picture in Activity C to play a memory game. With books closed, ask 1 *How many trees are there?* (two) 2 *Where's the robot?* (here) 3 *What colour is the balloon?* (blue) 4 *How many children are there?* (seven) 5 *What have Hugo, Mark and May got?* (a ball)

D Listen and say.

- Show the alphabet using Presentation plus or write it in large clear lower and upper case letters on the board. Talk about any differences between the English alphabet and learners' own alphabet in L1.
- Play the audio and point to each letter in turn. Learners listen.

12

- Say *Look at the alphabet!* Learners look at the alphabet in their books. Play the audio again. Learners listen and point. Play the alphabet again, a few letters at a time, for learners to repeat.

- Say the alphabet in open class. Learners trace the letter shapes in the air as they say the names.

- Practise individual letters your learners find difficult, e.g. *g, j, k, q, w, y, z*.

- Ask stronger learners *How do you spell your name?* They spell their name aloud.

E Choose and draw a blue line from the ruler to the pen. Ask and answer and draw a red line.

- Ask *Where's the ruler? Where's the pen?* Learners point. Point to the letters in the square.

- Learners each take a blue pen and draw a line over the letters from the picture of the ruler to the picture of the pen. They each choose their own route.

- Learners work in A and B pairs. Say to A learners: *Look at your blue line. Say the letters.* Say to B learners: *Listen and draw the line with a red pencil.* Learners then swap. Pairs then compare their blue and red lines.

Extension: Photocopiable 4a

Write the alphabet on the board and practise saying the letter names with the class. If necessary, have learners draw the letter shapes in the air as they say the names. Give each learner a photocopy of '4a The alphabet' (TB pages 50–51). Point to Activity 1. Start to read the first alphabet aloud as a class. Stop when you come to a missing letter and ask *What's next?* Ask a volunteer to write the missing letter on the board. Learners copy the letter.
Continue in this way until the alphabet is complete. Repeat for the capital letters. Stronger learners can complete the alphabets on their own.
Remind learners when to use capital letters, e.g. at the beginning of a sentence and for names of people and places, days of the week and months.
Point to the outlines in Activity 2 and ask *How many heads are there?* (four). Explain in L1 that learners need to draw portraits of four people who are important in their life, and write the names on the lines below.
Circulate and ask questions as learners work, e.g. *Is it a girl or a boy? What's his/her name? How do you spell that?*

Extension

Play a game to practise spelling. Say *This is a girl or boy in our class. Listen. What's his or her name?* Spell a learner's name letter by letter. Pause after each letter for learners to guess who it is. Ask *Do you know your classmate's name?* When a learner guesses correctly, say *Well done! Now you spell a name.*

F Listen and draw lines.

- Remind learners of the value discussion when they first read the story (see page 27) or discuss the value now for the first time.

- Learners look at the picture on Presentation plus or in their books. Ask *What animal is on the poster?* (a monkey) *Where's the purple book? Where are the green shoes?* (learners point)

- Practise pronunciation of the names and ask *Is it a girl or a boy?* Say *Alex is a boy's name. Alex is a girl's name, too.*

- Play the first part of the audio and do the example. Ask *What colour is May's bag?* (blue)

13

- Play the audio. Pause after each section for learners to draw lines. Play the audio once or twice more.

- Check answers in open class or use Presentation plus.

Tapescript:

Girl:	Hello! Are you our new teacher?	
Teacher:	Yes! What's your name?	
Girl:	Pat. But look! There's May!	
Teacher:	The girl with the blue school bag?	
Girl:	Yes, that's May! And that's her blue school bag.	

Can you see the line? This is an example. Now you listen and draw lines.

1	**Teacher:**	What's his name?
	Girl:	The boy with the red baseball cap?
	Teacher:	Yes!
	Girl:	The boy with the red baseball cap is Alex.
	Teacher:	Alex?
	Girl:	Yes.
2	**Girl:**	There's my friend, Lucy. She's got green shoes!
	Teacher:	They're great!
	Girl:	And she's got some new crayons. Lucy's really nice.
	Teacher:	That's good.
3	**Teacher:**	And the girl under the clock. What's her name?
	Girl:	Her name's Eva.
	Teacher:	Eva? OK.
	Girl:	She's got a new book.
	Teacher:	Wow!
4	**Girl:**	There's Mark.
	Teacher:	The boy on the yellow chair?
	Girl:	Yes. That's Mark's yellow chair.
	Teacher:	Good.
	Girl:	And what's your name?
	Teacher:	My name is Miss File!

Answers

Learners draw lines: Alex – boy with a red cap, Lucy – girl with green shoes, Eva – girl sitting under clock, Mark – boy sitting on yellow chair

---

G Read and choose the correct answer.

- Say *Look at picture 1. What's this? Is it a classroom?* (no) *A computer?* (yes) Say *Now you! Circle the correct answers.*

- Learners look, read and circle on their own or in pairs.
- Check answers in open class.
- You can do this activity again using pictures from the Image carousel, flashcards or pictures from magazines.

Extension

Give each learner a piece of paper. Draw four boxes on the board with space below the boxes for a word. Say *Now you draw four boxes. Draw four pictures.* Learners complete their drawings.
Say *Write 'It's a ...' sentences under your pictures. Write two correct sentences and two wrong sentences.*
In pairs, learners swap papers and circle the correct sentences.
They swap again to check answers.

Write. Ask and answer.

- Show your bag of items again. Ask *What's in my bag?* If learners remember an item, take it out. Ask *What's this? Tell me again!* Take it out and write the word on the board, e.g. *a ruler.*
- Look at Activity H. Ask *What's in my school bag?* Write an example on the board: *a pen.*
- Ask *What's in your school bag?* Show four fingers and say *Write four things.*
- Learners can tell the truth or write imagined things, e.g. *an ice cream, a teddy bear, a tablet.* Help with spelling if necessary.
- Ask a learner *What's in your school bag?* The learner answers *I've got ...* and reads their list.
- Ask *What's in your friend's school bag?* Say *Ask your friend and write.*
- Learners work in pairs. They take turns to ask and answer *What's in your school bag?* They listen and write. They can ask *How do you spell ...?* Then learners compare lists.
- Say *Close your books now.* Ask a confident learner *What's in your friend's school bag?* He/She tries to remember the four things. Check with the friend. Repeat with different learners. Say *Well done!*

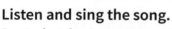

Listen and sing the song.

- Say *Look at the picture. Hugo and his friends sing a song about school. Let's look at the words.* Read the first verse. Stop at the missing words and ask *What's the word?* Learners guess (they don't write yet). Repeat for the other verses.
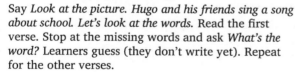
- Say *Listen and write the missing words.* Play the first verse of the song. Pause for learners to write the words. They compare their answers in pairs. Check answers.
- Check learners' understanding of *cool (= good), lesson, great, classmate (= child in the same class)* and *smile.*
- Play the song again.

Answers

1 school   **2** old   **3** cool   **4** books   **5** cool   **6** Yes

---

Tapescript:

See TB page 58

28

- Play the song several times. Learners join in.
- You can also listen to a version of this song without the words for learners to sing along to.

26

Let's Say! **Student's Book Page 74**

Say *Look at page 74. Listen.* Play the audio. Say *Let's say /ʌ/ duck.* Learners repeat. Say *Tell me more English words with /ʌ/.* Learners answer (e.g. bus, run). Repeat with sounds /ɒ/ *dog* (e.g. clock, song) and /ʊ/ *book* (e.g. good, put).

Let's have fun!

Play a game. Bingo!

Give each learner a photocopy of '4b Bingo!' (TB page 52). Ask *Can you see a book? A clock? A chair?*

Learners look at SB page 69 Activity 4. Say *Let's have fun! Let's play Bingo!*

In L1, say what to do: *Cut out the 12 pictures. Put them on your two Bingo! cards. You choose where. Get one card ready. Put the other one away for the moment. Listen to my sentences. Turn your picture over if it's on your Bingo card. When all your pictures are turned over, call 'Bingo!'*

Say *This book is great! That's my chair! Where's the spider? Cool hat! Wow! Balloons! A new ruler! Nice bike! It's a kite! Where's the box? Is that my pencil? Listen to the clock: tick, tock.*

You could give a small prize. Note that there may be more than one winner.

Repeat the game with the second game card. Read out the sentences in a different order, e.g. from the bottom of the list up.

Let's speak!

What's your name? Ask and answer.

Revise the alphabet. Learners close their books. Divide learners into four groups (A, B, C and D) and give each group a piece of paper. Ask each group to write the name you say on the paper. Say *Anna* to group A, *Tom* to group B, *Sue* to group C and *Pat* to group D. Groups remember, if they can, how to spell these names.

Check answers by asking a volunteer from each group to spell out their name from the story. Ask *Can you spell your name?* (learners answer) Write that question on the board. In pairs, learners then walk around and ask and answer the question with different classmates.

Home FUN booklet

➡ **Pages 10–11 school**
➡ **Pages 12–13 review**
➡ **Picture dictionary: school, places**

Go online

to practise your English
to listen to the audio recordings
to find more FUN activities!

5 What am I?

Main topics:	animals, the body and the face
Story summary:	A duck asks different animals how they are similar and different to find out what kind of animal it is.
Main grammar:	determiners (*a/an*), *can* (ability) and short answers
Main vocabulary:	*arm, big, body, crocodile, duck, ear, elephant, eye, face, fly, foot/feet, frog, funny, hippo, leg, long, monkey, mouth, nose, short, small, snake, sorry, spider, swim, tail, tree, walk*
Value:	Asking questions is good (*"Please tell me …"*)
Let's say!:	/l/ /r/ /m/ /n/
Practice for Starters:	Reading and Writing Part 3 (D), Listening Part 4 (F), Speaking Part 4 (I)

Equipment:

- ▶ audio: Story, Let's say!, F
- ↪ presentation **PLUS** flashcards
  (11 *elephant*, 7 *crocodile*, 20 *monkey*, 13 *frog*, 10 *duck*): Storytelling; (16 *hippo*, 25 *snake*): B; (29–40 *body*): D; (8 *dog*, 4 *cat*, 19 *lizard*, 26 *spider*): Let's have fun
- ↪ presentation **PLUS** Image carousel 23–33
  (5 pictures of animals, 6 pictures of activities) Photocopy 5 (TB page 53), one per learner: Let's have fun!

- crayons or colouring pens: B, F
- pieces of paper, one per learner: H
- large piece of card or paper, glue, crayons or colouring pens, pieces of card with phrases in large letters (for colouring in): *Excuse me! Please. Thank you. Sorry! Pardon?*, one per group of three or four learners: Let's have fun!

 ## Storytelling

Before listening

With books closed …

- Show pictures of the animals in the story (elephant, crocodile, monkey, frog, duck), from the Image carousel if available or use flashcards. Ask *What animal is this? Which is your favourite animal?* Learners answer.
- Review/Teach some parts of the body and *long, short*. Show an elephant and ask *Has it got small ears?* (no) *Has it got long legs?* (no) *Has it got a short tail?* (yes) *Has it got lots of teeth?* (no)
- Look at the first story picture without the story text on the Image carousel or with the story text in the book on page 36. Ask *What animals can you see?* (an elephant, a frog, a duck)
- Point to the other story pictures (with or without the text on the Image carousel or in the book) pages 37–39 and ask *What's this story about?* (Accept suggestions in English or L1.)
- Say *Now let's listen to the story.* Say *Let's look at page 36.*

Listening

With books open …

 15
- Play the audio or read the story. Learners listen.
- Play the audio or read the story again.
- Pause after page 36 and ask *Is the duck's body very big?* (no) *Has the duck got big ears?* (no)
- Pause after page 37 and ask *What animal is this?* (a crocodile) *Has the duck got teeth?* (no) *Has the duck got a long tail?* (no)
- Pause after page 38 and ask *What animal is this?* (a monkey) *Has the duck got a funny face?* (no) *Can the duck climb trees?* (no)
- Play the last part of the story. Ask *What colour are the duck's wings?* (brown) *What colour are the duck's feet?* (yellow) Mime swimming, walking and flying and ask *What can the duck do?* (swim, walk, fly)
- Say *The duck is happy! It says 'Yippee!'* Ask *Are you happy? Let's smile and say 'Yippee!'* Learners say *Yippee!*

After listening

- Talk about the story. Say *The duck asks a question. What does the duck ask the animals?* (What am I?) *What animal tells the duck its answer?* (a duck)
- Ask in L1 *Who do you ask if you have a question?* (friends, family, a teacher) *Do they also use the internet sometimes to find answers to questions?*

Value

- Look at page 36. Point to the first speech bubble in the story picture. Say *The duck says …* (Can you tell me, please?)
- Ask learners to say how they feel if someone tells them to do something and how they feel if someone asks them politely to do something (e.g. using *please* in their first language).
- Ask why it's important to be polite. Discuss how they might feel if they are with a friend who is rude to someone, or hear someone being impolite. In comparison, how do learners feel if they are with someone who is kind and respectful?
- Discuss the difference between saying *No!* and *No, thank you*, e.g. to a waiter in a café. Explain that in the UK, not saying *thank you* in this situation is impolite.

A Draw lines.

- Learners open their books and look at the pictures. They repeat the words.
- In pairs or small groups, learners say the words.
- Do the example. Say *Draw lines from the words to the correct picture.*
- Check answers in open class or use Presentation plus.

Answers

1 a   2 c   3 d   4 b

B Which animals does the duck talk to? Choose and colour the path yellow.

- Learners look at the path. Ask *How many animals can you see?* (eight) Learners say the animals. Show flashcards or draw pictures to review/teach *hippo* and *snake*.
- Ask *Which animals does the duck talk to in the story?* Say *Colour the path yellow.* Learners colour the path from the duck to the animals the duck talks to, in the correct order.
- Check answers using Presentation plus or the Student's Book.

Answers

Learners colour the path from the duck to the elephant, crocodile, monkey and duck.

Extension

Learners choose an animal and prepare a presentation. They draw a picture of the animal or find a photograph. Write a model on the board: *Tigers are orange and black. They have got four legs. Tigers can run. They can swim.* Learners write their presentations.

C Who is correct? Read and write.

- Check understanding of *correct*. Say *One child is <u>right</u> about the duck. This child is <u>correct</u>. Two children are <u>wrong</u> about the duck. They are <u>not</u> correct.*
- In pairs, learners read the speech bubbles. Ask *Who is correct?* (Sam) Learners write *Sam* on the line.
- Say *The duck says 'Please tell me'.* Give more examples of when we might use *please* because we want someone to do something, e.g. *Please help me! Please be quiet! Please answer my question.*

Extension

Ask learners to say other sentences with *Please*, e.g. *Please stand up, Please spell your name.*

D Look at the pictures. Look at the letters. Write the words.

- Write *an elephant* and *a crocodile* on the board. Ask why we write *an* before *elephant* and *a* before *crocodile*. Say in L1 that it's difficult to say *a* before a word beginning *a, e, i, o* or *u*.
- Review/Teach parts of the body using body flashcards. Point to parts of your body and say *This is (a/an) …* (eye, ear, nose, mouth, head, hair, face, arm, hand, leg, foot) Learners say the word in chorus.
- Learners stand up, listen and point. Say *Where are your eyes? Point to an ear! Now point to your nose! Where's your mouth? Point to a tooth! Where are your arms? Point to a leg! Now point to a foot! Where's your hair? Point to your feet! Put up your hands!*
- Learners look at the pictures and jumbled letters in Activity D. Do the example. Learners solve the jumbled words in pairs.
- Check answers in open class. Ask different pairs to spell the words.

Answers

1 ear   2 leg   3 body   4 foot   5 mouth

Test tip: STARTERS
Reading and Writing (Part 3)

✔ In the test, learners look at five jumbled words with picture clues. Remind learners that they use the letters given and can cross out the letters in pencil as they use them. They can count the letters in the jumbled word and their answer.

➔ Write jumbled words on the board for them to solve: *efac* (face), *dahn* (hand), *osen* (nose), *tlia* (tail). Learners can also make jumbled words for each other.

26 | 🔊 *Let's say!* **Student's Book Page 75**

Say *Look at page 75. Listen.* Play the audio. Say *Let's say*
/ʌ/ *lemonade.* Learners repeat. Say *Tell me more English*
words with /ʌ/. Learners answer (e.g. leg, long). Repeat
with sounds /r/ *robot* (e.g. ruler, run), /m/ *monkey* (e.g.
mouth, mum) and /n/ *nose* (e.g. Nick, no).

Read and choose the crocodile's answer.

* Ask *In the story, which animal asks 'Can you climb*
  trees?' (the monkey) *What does the duck say?* (No,
  I can't!) Ask different learners *Can you climb trees?*
  Encourage learners to say *Yes, I can.* Write on the
  board *Yes, I can* and *No, I can't.*

* Review/Teach *run, walk, talk, fly, swim, jump.* Use the
  pictures on the Image carousel, if available. Learners
  say the words and mime. Ask different learners *Can*
  you run? Can you swim? They use short answers.

* Ask *What does the crocodile answer?* Do the example.
  Learners read and circle.

* Check answers using Presentation plus or in open
  class.

Answers

2 Yes, I can. **3** Yes, I can. **4** No, I can't.

Listen and colour.

Revise colours. Ask *What colour is the …?* questions
about objects in the classroom.

Ask *Which animal has got a funny face in the story?*
(the monkey) *What can a monkey do?* (climb trees)
Do monkeys like bananas? (yes)

* Learners look at the picture. Ask *How many monkeys*
  are there? (five) Learners write *5* under the picture.
  Ask *Can you see the green monkey? Where's the green*
  monkey? (learners point) Ask *What other animals can*
  you see? (a duck and a spider)

* Play the first section of the audio. Ask *Where's the red*
  monkey? (learners point)

16

---

* Say *Listen and colour.* Make sure that each learner has
  crayons or colouring pens. Remind learners that they
  don't need to finish colouring each monkey.

* Play the rest of the audio. Learners listen and colour
  the other monkeys. Play the audio again if necessary.

* Check answers using Presentation plus or in open
  class. Ask, e.g. *What colour is the monkey in the water?*

* Learners can finish colouring for homework.

Answers

monkey with bananas – red
monkey in the water – yellow
monkey in the flowers – blue

Tapescript:

1	Boy:	I love bananas.
	Woman:	Me too. Look! One monkey has got some bananas. Colour that monkey.
	Boy:	OK.
	Woman:	Colour it red.
	Boy:	Colour it red?
	Woman:	Yes.
2	Boy:	One monkey is in the water!
	Woman:	Yes! Colour that monkey.
	Boy:	OK.
	Woman:	Colour it yellow.
	Boy:	Sorry? Yellow?
	Woman:	Yes, please.
3	Boy:	And one monkey is in the flowers!
	Woman:	Yes! Colour that monkey, now.
	Boy:	OK. What colour?
	Woman:	Colour it blue.
	Boy:	Blue?
	Woman:	Yes, please. That's great! Thank you!

Test tip: STARTERS
Listening (Part 4)

✔ In Part 4, learners need to colour five of the seven
  objects in a picture. The objects are always the same,
  e.g. seven balls or seven cakes. Learners will hear
  where the object is and which colour to use. One
  object will be coloured already and one will not need
  to be coloured.

➔ Practise *in* and *on.* Say *Find your red crayon. Put your*
  crayon on your head. Put your crayon in your bag.
  Now put your crayon on your desk. Use other Starters
  prepositions: *behind, between, in front of, under* and
  next to in the same way, as learners first learn them.

G Read and choose the correct answer.

- Look at the example. Say *Monkeys love bananas! That's the correct answer!*
- Learners read the sentences and circle the correct words.
- Check answers in open class or use Presentation plus.

Answers
2 arms **3** swim **4** hands **5** walk **6** run

Test tip: STARTERS
All parts

✔ Learners should now know: *bird, cat, crocodile, dog, duck, elephant, fish, frog, giraffe, hippo, lizard, monkey, mouse (mice), snake, spider* and *tiger.* Other Starters animal words: *bear, bee, chicken, cow, donkey, goat, horse, jellyfish, sheep* and *zebra.*

➜ Write ten known animal words on the board. In L1, tell learners to choose to be one of these animals and to keep this a secret.

In open class, ask one or two learners about their animal. Write some example questions on the board: *What colour are you? How many legs have you got? Can you swim?*

Divide learners into groups of four. Learners take turns to guess the animals.

H Look, read and write.

- Learners look at the picture. In L1, ask which two animals this creature looks like (a crocodile and an elephant).
- Learners look at the example and then write answers.
- Check answers with Presentation plus or in open class.

Answers
2 green and brown **3** yellow **4** yes **5** yes **6** no

Extension

Play a memory game. Learners look at the picture in Activity H for 20 seconds. Say *Close your books.* Divide learners into teams of four.
Ask questions about the picture: *1 How many feet has the animal got?* (four) *2 What colour are its ears?* (grey) *3 Has it got long teeth?* (yes) *4 Has it got a small mouth?* (no) *5 Has it got a short body?* (no) *6 Has the girl got short hair?* (no) *7 What colour is the boy's T-shirt?* (red) *8 What colour are the girl's shoes?* (blue)
In teams, learners write the answers.
Check answers in open class.

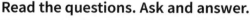

I Read the questions. Ask and answer.

- Point to the duck and ask *What's this?* (a duck) *Where is this duck? In some …* (water) *What colour is its head, body and tail?* (yellow/orange) *Can it swim?* (yes) *Have you or your brothers or sisters got a toy duck?* (yes/no) *What's your favourite animal?* Learners answer.
- Say *Let's read the duck's questions.* Ask a learner to read the first question. The learner chooses a friend to answer. Continue in this way with the three other questions.
- Learners then ask and answer in pairs. They can use a 'duck' voice for the questions.

5 *Let's have fun!*

Play an animal game.

Give each learner a photocopy of '5 Animals' (TB page 53).

Point to the three pictures and ask *What are these animals?* (an elephant, a crocodile, a monkey) For each animal, ask *How do you spell (elephant)?* Ask different learners to write the words on the board. Learners copy the words under the pictures.

Say *Four animals from the story aren't here. What are they?* (duck, frog, snake and hippo)

Say *Draw the animals and write the words.* Learners draw and write.

Ask *Can you draw more animals?* Show the flashcards for *dog, cat, lizard, spider* to help learners remember.

Point to the last box and say *Now you! Choose an animal and write the word.* Learners complete the grid.

Ask *Where's the (monkey)? Where's an animal with eight legs? Where's an animal with big ears? Where's an animal with two legs?* Learners point to the correct pictures.

Learners cut out the cards. In pairs, they put their matching cards together and play a game, e.g. Snap! or Pelmanism.

5 *Let's speak!*

Play a game. Who is it?

In pairs, learners talk about a classmate for other learners to guess, e.g. *A girl. Brown hair. Green eyes.* The partner guesses the name of the classmate. The learner says *Yes. Well done!* or *No.*

🏠 **Home FUN booklet**
➡ **Pages 14–15 animals**
➡ **Picture dictionary: animals, the body and face, sports**

Go online

to practise your English
to listen to the audio recordings
to find more FUN activities!

Grandma's glasses

6

Main topics:	the home, family
Story summary:	A grandmother can't find her glasses at home. Members of the family help her to find them.
Main grammar:	prepositions of place (*in, on, under, next to*), *This is … / These are …*, questions with *What/Where/Who*
Main vocabulary:	*armchair, bedroom, computer, cupboard, desk, drive, find, glasses, handbag, hat, home, Jill, kitchen, lamp, living room, look, old, ride, rug, sock, sofa, TV*
Value:	Helping others ("*I can help!*")
Let's say!:	/k/ /g/
Practice for Starters:	Reading and Writing Part 3 (F), Reading and Writing Part 5 (G), Listening Part 4 (H), Speaking Part 1 (I)

Equipment:	• ▶ audio: Story, Let's say!, H	• objects from the story: glasses, handbag, coat, toothbrush, pair of socks, ruler (optional): Storytelling, A
	• ↪ presentation **PLUS** flashcards (55 *socks*, 167 *ruler*, 176 *bike*, 213 *car*): Storytelling; (125 *cupboard*, 143 *table*, 124 *computer*, 144 *television*, 115 *armchair*): C, D; (129 *flowers*, 46 *glasses*, 56 *trousers*): F	• crayons or colouring pens: F, H , I • props for role play: glasses, hat, book: G Extension • Photocopy 6 (TB page 54), one per learner (optional): Let's speak!
	• ↪ presentation **PLUS** Image carousel 34–37 (4 pictures of glasses in different positions)	• magazines with pictures of rooms and furniture, piece of paper per learner, scissors, glue, colouring pencils or pens (optional): Let's have fun!

 Storytelling

Before listening

With books closed …

- Before class, put some glasses in a handbag. Say *Oh dear! Where are my glasses?* Look under learners' chairs, in school bags, etc. Ask *Are they under your chair?* (no) *Are they behind the door?* (no)
- Look in the handbag and say *Here they are! They're in my handbag.* Hold up the glasses and the handbag and say the two words.
- Ask, in L1, *Who wears glasses in our class? Do you sometimes lose them?*
- Review/Teach *coat, toothbrush, socks* and *ruler* using objects, or flashcards and pictures. Show flashcards of a bike and a car or draw them. Learners say the words.
- Say *These things are in today's story. Can you guess what happens?* Learners give ideas in L1.
- Look at the first story pictures without the story text on the Image carousel or with the story text in the book on page 44 and ask *Who's got a bike?* (the old woman) *Who is she?* (Grandma) Ask *Who is next to the door?* (Mum, Dad, a boy and a girl)
- Learners look at the other story picture (with or without the text on the Image carousel or in the book) pages 45–47. Ask *What hasn't Grandma got?* (her glasses) Explain the meaning of *find*.
- Say *Now let's listen to the story.* Say *Let's look at page 44.*

Listening

With books open …

17

- Play the audio or read the story. Learners listen.
- Play the audio or read the story again.
- Pause after page 44 and ask *What four things has Grandma got?* (handbag, coat, toothbrush, bike) *What are the names of the children?* (Jill and Tom) *Does Tom find the glasses?* (no) *What does he find?* (his robot)
- Pause after page 45 and ask *Does Jill find Grandma's glasses?* (no) *What does she find?* (her ruler) *Does Mum find the glasses?* (no) *What does she find?* (her socks)
- Pause after page 46 and ask *Can Grandma ride her bike?* (no) *That's right! She can't …* (see)
- Play the last part of the story. Ask *Where are Grandma's glasses?* (on her head)

After listening

- Encourage learners to talk about the story, in L1 if necessary. Ask *Who finds the glasses?* (Grandma) *Does she go home in the car?* (no, she rides her bike)
- Ask in L1 *Do you lose things sometimes? Where do you usually find them?*

 Value

- Look at page 44. Point to the speech bubble in the story picture. Say *Tom says ...* (I can help!)
- In L1, ask *How does Grandma feel when she loses her glasses?* (worried, upset) Say *The family help Grandma.*
- Personalise the idea of helping. Ask *Do you help your friends and family? How can you help at home?*

 Draw lines.

- Learners look at the pictures. Ask different learners questions about the house, car and computer pictures, e.g. *Do you live in a house? How many windows are there in this/your house? Has your family got a car? What colour is your car? Have you got a computer at home? What can you do on a computer?* Learners answer.
- In pairs, learners say the words.
- Say *Draw the lines from the words to the correct picture.*
- Check answers in open class or use Presentation plus.

Answers

1 d   **2** e   **3** c   **4** a   **5** b

 Look and read the questions. Write one-word answers.

- Hold up your pencil and ask *What's this? It's a ...* (pencil) *What colour is it?* (red) Put the pencil on your desk and ask *Where's the pencil? On the ...* (desk) Give your pencil to a learner and ask *Who's got my pencil?* (learners answer)
- In pairs, learners read the questions and write one-word answers. If necessary, they can check spelling in the story.

Answers

1 glasses   **2** Tom   **3** ruler   **4** Mum   **5** head   **6** bike

Test tip: STARTERS
Reading and Writing (Part 5)

✔ Learners are asked five questions about a picture story. Learners write one word either on its own or to complete a short phrase.

➜ Write questions about the first picture from the story on the board: *How many people are there?* (five) *What animal can you see? a* (cat) *What colour is the car?* (blue) *Who is behind Tom?* (Mum) Learners copy and answer.

 Write a, b or c in the boxes.

- Point to the pictures and ask *What are these?* Learners answer: *a cupboard, a cushion, a computer, a TV, an armchair, a table.* Write the words on the board and practise pronunciation.
- Show flashcards and/or pictures of the furniture in different orders. Learners say *It's a/an ...*
- Point to the people in Activity C. Ask *Who's this?* Learners read the names. Point to the first picture. Ask *Who looks here?* (Tom) *Which letter is Tom?* (a)

- Learners look at the pictures and write the correct letters.
- Check answers in open class or using Presentation plus.

Answers

1 a   **2** c   **3** b   **4** b   **5** c   **6** a

Extension

Play a game to practise furniture. Say *Look, listen and remember.* Show six to eight flashcards (or pictures) of furniture from a living room. Say *In my living room there's a big blue sofa. There's an armchair. There's a TV. There's a computer. There's a small brown table. And there's a cupboard.* Repeat.
Then ask *What's in my living room? Can you remember?* Learners write all the words they can remember. Check answers.

 Draw lines.

- Use flashcards to review/teach *clock* and review the furniture from the previous activity.
- Learners look at the picture. Ask *What room is this?* (living room) *What can you see?*
- Do the example. Say *Draw lines from the words to the correct part of the picture.*
- Check answers in open class or use Presentation plus.

Look and read the questions. Write one-word answers.

- Say *Now read the four questions.* Ask *What are the answers? Numbers?* (no) *Colours?* (yes) *There's one example. What colour is the armchair?* (orange)
- Say *Now you! Write the answers.*

Answers

2 brown   **3** blue   **4** yellow

 26 *Let's say!* **Student's Book Page 74**

Say *Look at page 74. Listen.* Play the audio. Say *Let's say /k/ **c**omputer.* Learners repeat. Say *Tell me more English words with /k/.* Learners answer (e.g. cupboard, kitchen). Repeat with sound /g/ **g**reen (e.g. Grandma, glasses).

 Read and choose the correct answer.

- Review/Teach *in, on, next to* and *under* using the flashcards, the Image carousel or objects in the classroom.

- A learner thinks of an object in the classroom. Ask the learner questions to guess the object: *What colour is it? Where is it? Is it on the wall? Is it on your desk? Is it under the window? Is it the computer?* When you have guessed, write the questions you asked on the board. Repeat the game with two more learners. The class guess.
- Learners play the same game in pairs.
- Look at Activity E. Point to the example and ask *Where's the cat?* (in the cupboard) Learners point to the correct picture. In pairs, they complete the sentence.
- Check answers using Presentation plus or in open class.

Answers
2 on **3** under **4** next to **5** on **6** under

Extension
Say *Close your eyes.* Hide objects, e.g. your watch, your ruler and your pen, in the classroom. Say *I can't find my watch! Where is it?* Learners say *I can help!* Learners guess where the item is. Write guesses on the board, e.g. *in the cupboard – Sara, under your chair – Alvaro, next to your desk – Mariano.* Learners look where they guessed and bring you the item. Say *Great! Thank you.*

F Look at the pictures. Look at the letters. Write and colour.

- Revise *this* and *these*. Show flashcards or point to items. Learners say sentences, e.g. *This is a table. These are flowers.* Explain in L1 that we use *these* for *These are glasses* and *These are trousers* because glasses have two lenses and trousers have two legs!
- Ask *What colour is Grandma's hat in the story?* (blue) Look at the example and ask *Is this Grandma's hat?* (yes) *How do you spell 'hat'?* (H–A–T)
- Learners complete sentences 2–5 and colour the pictures.
- Check answers in open class.

Answers
2 ruler **3** robot **4** socks **5** glasses

Extension

Make a space in the classroom. Use four chairs to be the car in the story.
Ask six confident learners to be Dad, Mum, Jill, Tom, Grandma and the cat. Grandma has a hat and glasses and Jill has a book. Learners look at the picture at the top of SB page 47. They stand or sit in the same places (Dad, Grandma and the children in the car, and Mum and the cat next to the car).
They act out the scene:
Mum: Bye!
Cat: Meow!
Grandma: [mimes feeling hot]
  It's hot!
  [takes off her hat]
Tom and Jill: Your glasses are on your head!
Grandma: [takes glasses off her head]
  Fantastic!
  [everyone laughs]

G Look, read and write the number.

- Look at the example. Say *All the answers are numbers.*
- In pairs, learners ask and answer the questions. They write the answers on the lines. Remind learners to write figures, not the words.

Answers
2 1 **3** 6 **4** 2

Extension
For stronger learners, do a 'spot the difference' between Activity G and the story picture at the top of SB page 47. Say *In the story Grandma's hair is … What colour?* (grey) *But in this picture Grandma's hair is …* (white) *In the story, Grandma's glasses are purple, but in this picture they are …* (yellow) *In the story, Jill hasn't got a book, but in this picture she …* (has got a book) *In the story the cat is next to the car. In this picture the cat is …* (behind the car) *In the story, Grandma's got an orange bag. In this picture she's got …* (flowers) *In the story Grandma's hat is on her head. But in this picture it's …* (in her hand)

H Listen and colour.

- Learners look at the picture. Say *This is the end of the story. Where's Grandma?* (on her bike) *Has she got her glasses?* (yes) *How many hats can you see?* (seven)
- Make sure each learner has crayons, including red, yellow, pink and purple. Say *Listen and colour the hats.*
- Play the audio and pause after the first hat. Ask *What colour is the hat under the car?* (pink)
- Play the audio. Learners colour the hats.
- Learners compare drawings and then listen again.
- Learners can finish colouring at the end of the lesson or for homework.

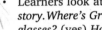
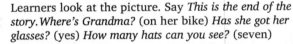
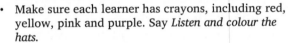

18

Answers
hat under car – pink   hat in Grandma's bag – yellow hat in Dad's hand – purple   hat on tree – red

Tapescript:		
1	Man:	One hat is under the car. Look!
	Girl:	Under the car! Oh yes.
	Man:	Colour that hat pink, please.
	Girl:	Pink! OK!
2	Man:	There's a hat in Grandma's bag. Can you see it?
	Girl:	The hat in Grandma's bag? Yes, I can see it.
	Man:	Great! Colour it yellow.
	Girl:	Yellow. OK.
3	Man:	Look! Dad's got a hat. It's in his hand.
	Girl:	Oh, yes! One hat is in Dad's hand.
	Man:	That's right. Colour his hat purple.
	Girl:	Purple. OK!

4	Man:	And now the hat on the tree!
	Girl:	The hat on the tree! OK! What colour?
	Man:	Red, please.
	Girl:	OK. It's red now.
	Man:	Thank you!

Test tip: STARTERS
Listening (Part 4)

✔ For Listening Part 4, learners must know the colours *blue, brown, green, grey, orange, pink, purple, red* and *yellow*. They will not be asked to colour an object black or white. Tell learners that their colouring does not have to be complete or very neat.

→ Describe a picture for learners to draw: *Draw a house. Colour it brown. Draw a tree next to the house. Draw five apples on the tree. Colour the apples red. Draw a car under the tree. Colour the car yellow. Draw some flowers next to the car. Colour the flowers purple.*
Learners compare pictures.

Draw the things in your room. Then talk and point.

- Point to the picture of the room and the smaller pictures. Ask *Which room is this?* (a bedroom) Ask *What can you see?* (a rug, a TV, a bed, an armchair, a desk, a lamp, a cupboard) Say *Draw the things in your room.* Explain in L1 that learners can draw the items wherever they want in the room. They don't colour them. Circulate and ask *Where's the TV? Where's the lamp?* etc. Learners point or answer, e.g. *On the desk.*

- Then learners work in pairs. Learner A asks questions about the items in Learner B's picture (*Where's the ...?*) and Learner B points. They swap roles.

- Learners colour the pictures for homework. In the next class they compare their pictures. They ask *What colour's the (armchair)?*

Let's have fun!

Make a picture and write.

Learners look at SB page 70 Activity 6. Say *Let's have fun! Let's make a picture!*

Learners choose a room (bedroom, living room or kitchen). They cut out magazine pictures of furniture and objects from this room, and stick them on an A4 page to make a room collage. They can use the example on SB page 70 as a model.

Learners label the furniture and objects, e.g. *door, red sofa, pink flowers, big window, nice clock, black TV.* Learners show and talk about their collage.

Display the collages if possible.

Let's speak!

Where is it? Ask and answer. Colour.

Give each learner a photocopy of '6 Where is it?' (TB page 54). Ask *Is this an old house/flat or a new house/flat?* (new) *How many rooms can you see?* (two) *What can you see?* (a bed, a mat, an armchair, a sofa) Revise the names of these rooms (bedroom and living room) and others in the home.

Learners colour the small pictures and 'place' these in one of the two rooms. They can do this by drawing lines to show which thing goes in each room, by copying the pictures and drawing these items in each room or by cutting the pictures out and placing or gluing them in each room. Learners then add three or four details of their own choice, e.g. a ball, a toy, a book, a radio.

Ask two or three learners *What ...? What colour ...? What's in/on ...?* questions, e.g. *What colour's the cupboard? What's in the bedroom? What's on the bed?*

In pairs, learners then ask and answer questions about the location of objects in each other's pictures, e.g. *Lamp? On the rug.*

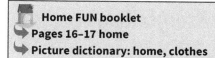

Extension

Learners draw their own homes or rooms and describe them to others in the class, e.g. *In our living room, there's / we've got a yellow sofa and a big TV.* Alternatively, groups could find pictures of rooms in magazines and cut them out to make a 'home' collage. They could label the furniture they can see in each room or features of the rooms (e.g. *door, window, floor*). If possible, display these drawings or collages around the room.

Home FUN booklet
Pages 16–17 home
Picture dictionary: home, clothes

Go online

to practise your English
to listen to the audio recordings
to find more FUN activities!

Let's go there now!

Main topics:	sports, places
Story summary:	Two children talk about what sports they like and dislike.
Main grammar:	*Do you like …? Yes, I do. / No, I don't., Which …? Who …?*
Main vocabulary:	*afternoon, Alice, badminton, baseball, baseball cap, bat, beach, evening, favourite, fishing, go, good, home, live, lunch, Matt, now, park, sea, shell, skateboarding, tennis, tennis racket*
Value:	appreciating differences and similarities (*"Do you like …? Yes, I do. / No, I don't."*)
Let's say!:	/j/ /w/
Practice for Starters:	Listening Part 2 (F), Speaking Part 3 (E)

Equipment:	audio: Story, D, Let's say!, F	• sports equipment: basketball ball / tennis ball / badminton/tennis racket or hockey stick / skateboard / towel: Storytelling, A, G
	(→) (presentation **PLUS** flashcards) (195 *tennis racket*, 181 *football*, 194 *table tennis*, 173 *basketball*, 174 *bat*, 203 *ball*): Storytelling; (149 *playground*, 150 *shop*, 148 *park*, 175 *beach*): C; (195 *tennis*, 181 *football*): E	• small strip of paper for each learner: Storytelling Extension (Value) • sports bag: G • crayons or colouring pens: G • A4 paper, scissors, glue, crayons or pens, magazine pictures of sports: Let's have fun!
	(→) (presentation **PLUS** Image carousel 38–41) (2 pictures of shops, 2 pictures of sports)	• Photocopy 7 (TB page 55), one per learner (optional): Let's speak!

Storytelling

Before listening

With books closed …

- Show sports equipment or use the flashcards, e.g. a tennis racket, a football, table tennis bats, a basketball. Say *This is my racket/ball/bat. What's the sport?* (e.g. tennis) Learners pass the item around. Hold up the tennis racket and ask *Who likes tennis?* (learners put up their hands) Repeat with other equipment.
- Write *sports shop* on the board. Show photographs of the inside of a sports shop from the Image carousel. Ask *Can you see the tennis rackets / T-shirts / baseball caps / footballs?*
- Say *Some sports are in today's story. Can you guess which ones?* Learners guess.
- Look at the story pictures (with or without the text on the Image carousel or in the book) pages 52–55. Say *Tell me about the sports in the story. Look at the pictures.* Learners look and guess (badminton, horse riding, tennis, baseball, skateboarding and swimming).
- Ask *How many children are in the story?* (two) Look at the second story picture (with or without the text on the Image carousel or in the book) page 52 and ask *Are they sisters?* (no) *They are …* (friends)
- Point to the picture of the sports shop on the Image carousel or in the book page 53 and ask *Where are the children?* (the sports shop)
- Point to the picture of the children at the playground on the Image carousel or in the book page 54 and ask *Where are they now?* (the playground) Point to the picture on the Image carousel or in the book page 55 and ask *Where are they now?* (the park)
- Say *Now let's listen to the story.* Say *Let's look at page 52.*

Listening

With books open …

19

- Play the audio or read the story. Learners listen.
- Play the audio or read the story again.
- Pause after page 52 and ask *Where do Matt and Alice live?* (next to the beach / in Sea Street)
- Pause after page 54 and ask *What colour is Matt's skateboard?* (red) *What colour is Alice's skateboard?* (grey)
- Play the last part of the story. Point to the last page and say *Look at Matt. He's in the water. What does Alice say?* (Do you like swimming?) Ask *Why?* (learners answer in L1)

After listening

- Encourage learners to talk about the story (in L1 if necessary). Ask *What sport does Matt do at the park?* (skateboarding) *What does Alice like doing at the park?* (skateboarding) Say *Yes, Matt and Alice like skateboarding.*
- Ask *What sports in the story do you like? What sports do your friends like?*

Value

- Look at page 53. Point to the speech bubbles in the story picture. Say *Matt says … (Do you like baseball?) Alice says … (No, I don't.)* In L1, ask *Do Alice and Matt like the same sport?* (no)
- Say *Look at the picture of Matt and Alice in the playground. Matt says 'I go skateboarding in the park.' What does Alice say?* (Me too!) Say *Matt and Alice say this when they do the same thing.*
- Say *Matt and Alice are different. Are they friends?* (yes) Say *Everyone is different and they like different things. It's good that people can be the same and can be different.*
- Personalise the idea of appreciating differences. Ask learners *Does your friend like different things? What things?*

Extension

Write on the board *I like …* Learners complete the sentence about something they like (e.g. a food, a sport, an animal, a place, a book, a musician/band) on a piece of paper.
Learners memorise their sentence. They walk around the room. Say *Stop!* Learners make a pair with the person next to them. Learner A says his/her sentence, e.g. *I like books.* Learner B replies *Me too!* or *I don't!* If they answer *Me too!* they swap papers.
Say *Go!* and learners walk again. Repeat the activity so learners speak to five people.

Extension

Stronger learners write about themselves and a friend. Write a model text on the board:
My friend (Da Xia) likes tennis and drawing. So do I.

A Draw lines.

- Ask *How many … ? Have you got … ?* and *What colour … ?* questions about the pictures in Activity A, e.g. *How many sports can you see here?* (six) *How many rackets are there?* (two) *Have you got a skateboard / tennis racket / swimming cap?* (yes/no) *What colour is your/this skateboard?* (purple/pink) *What colour is your/this swimming cap?* (blue)
- Say *Draw lines from the words to the correct picture.*
- Check answers in open class or use Presentation plus.

Answers

1 f   2 e   3 c   4 b   5 d   6 a

B Read and put a tick (✔) in the boxes.

- Look at question 1. Ask *Does Alice like horse riding?* (yes) *Does Matt like horse riding?* (no) *Who likes horse riding?* (Alice) Point to the tick. Say *Tick here.* Point to the empty box and ask *Do we put a tick here?* (no)
- Say *Read and tick. Think – who likes this: Alice, Matt or Alice and Matt? You can tick two.*
- Learners read the sentences and tick one or both boxes.
- Check answers using Presentation plus or on the board.

Answers

2 Alice   3 Matt   4 Alice   5 Matt   6 Alice and Matt

C Where's Matt? Look, read and write the number.

- Show flashcards of *playground, shop, park* and *beach,* and pictures of *home* and *bus stop,* or use the pictures in Activity C. Learners say what's in each picture, e.g. *(This is a) playground.*

- Mime putting on sun cream. Ask *Where am I?* Learners guess (beach). Repeat with other places: looking at your watch and waiting (bus stop), skateboarding (park), choosing a tennis racket and opening a wallet/purse to pay for it (sports shop), climbing (playground), sleeping (home).
- Say *Where's Matt?* Learners look at the pictures in Activity C, read the sentences and write the correct numbers in the boxes.
- Learners check in pairs.
- Check in open class or use Presentation plus.
- Ask *Which is your favourite place?*

Answers

Beach 2, Sports shop 5, Park 4,
Bus stop 6, Playground 1, Home 3

D Listen and draw lines.

- Ask *Which sport do Alice and Matt do in the park?* (skateboarding) Say *Look at Activity D. Let's read the names.* Learners repeat *Alice, Sue, Matt, Grace, Ben.*
- Say *Point to (Grace).* Learners point. Repeat with the other names.
- Say *Let's say the colours.* Learners say the colours of the skateboards in order. (red (and white), grey (and pink), orange (and yellow), blue (and green), purple (and black), green) Ask *Where's the skateboard with flowers? Where's the skateboard with a sun?* (learners point)
- Say *Which is your favourite skateboard?* In pairs, learners choose. Ask different pairs *What colour is your favourite skateboard?*
- Say *Listen and draw lines.*

 20

- Play the audio. Learners listen and draw lines from the children to the skateboards.
- Check answers in open class or use Presentation plus.
- Say *Please close your books.* Say *Tell me the names again.* (Alice, Sue, Matt, Grace, Ben) Ask *Can you spell the names?* Write the names on the board as learners spell. Ask *How do you spell Alice? Can you spell Sue?*

Tapescript:

Woman:	Hello, Alice! Which is your skateboard?
Alice:	That one! It's grey.
Woman:	Oh … Alice! It's got a funny face on it!
Alice:	That's right!
Woman:	And hi, Sue! Which is your skateboard?
Sue:	My skateboard is purple. Look!
Woman:	Oh, yes! With the black feet on it! I love your skateboard, Sue.
Sue:	Ha ha!
Woman:	Hi, Matt!
Matt:	Hello! My skateboard is red.
Woman:	Red? That's my favourite colour. It's a really great skateboard, Matt.
Matt:	Thanks!
Woman:	And hello, Grace! Which is your skateboard?
Grace:	My skateboard is blue.
Woman:	I love the flowers on your skateboard, Grace!
Grace:	Me too!
Ben:	I'm here too!
Woman:	Oh, yes. Hello, Ben. Which is your skateboard?
Ben:	Orange is my favourite colour. My skateboard is orange.
Woman:	Wow! It's fantastic, Ben.
Ben:	Yes, it is!

26))) **Let's say! Student's Book Page 79**

Say *Look at page 75. Listen.* Play the audio. Say *Let's say* /j/ *yellow.* Learners repeat. Say *Tell me more English words with* /j/. Learners answer (e.g. yes, you). Repeat with sound /w/ *white* (e.g. water, which).

E Read and put a tick (✔) in the box. Now ask and answer.

- Draw a happy and a sad smiley on the board.
- Show a flashcard or a picture of a sport you like, e.g. tennis. Write *tennis* on the board. Say *I like tennis.* Put a tick under the happy smiley. Show a picture of a sport you don't like, e.g. football. Write *football* on the board. Say *I don't like football.* Put a tick under the sad smiley.
- Learners look at the list of sports in Activity E. Say *What sports do you like? Read and put a tick in the box under the happy face. What sports don't you like? Put a tick in the box under the sad face.* Learners tick.
- Ask different learners *Do you like baseball? Do you like tennis? Do you like football?* Learners answer, e.g. *Yes, (I do.) / No, (I don't.).*

- Ask different learners, e.g. *Who do you play baseball with? Where do you go swimming? What colour is your football? Do you like horses / eating fish / watching sport on TV?*
- In pairs, learners ask and answer about the sports.

> **Test tip: STARTERS**
> *Speaking (Part 4)*
>
> ✔ Learners will need to answer three open questions with question words *What, Where, Who, How many* and *How old*, e.g. *What's your friend's name? Who do you sit next to in class? What's your favourite sport? Where do you play with your friends?*
> → Write three open, personalised questions on the board, e.g. *What sports do you like? Who do you play sports with? Where do you play sports?* In pairs, learners ask and answer questions about themselves.

F Listen and write a name or a number.

- Say *Let's look at the picture. What can you see?* (a girl / a tennis racket) *What sport does she like?* (tennis) Say *Look at number 1.* Ask *What is this girl's name?* (Kim)
- Say *Listen. A girl is talking to her dad. She's telling her dad about Kim.* Point to the questions and say *The answers are names or numbers.*
- Say *Let's say the alphabet.* Learners say the alphabet in chorus. Ask *Can you spell Kim?* (yes) *How do you spell Kim?* (K-I-M) Say *Great! Well done.* Ask *Now, how do you spell school?* (S-C-H-O-O-L)
- Say *Let's read the questions.* Five learners read questions 3–7. Check understanding and pronunciation of *Mrs.*
- Play the audio, pausing for learners to write. Repeat.
- Learners compare answers in pairs.
- Check using Presentation plus or in open class.

21

Tapescript:

Look at the picture.

Listen and look.

There are two examples.

Girl:	Look, Dad! That's my friend.
Man:	Oh! What's her name?
Girl:	Her name's Kim.
Man:	Sorry?
Girl:	Her name's Kim. K-I-M!
Man:	How old is she?
Girl:	She's eight. She's eight, like me.
Man:	OK.

Can you see the answers? Now you listen and write a name or a number.

3	Man:	Where is your friend's school?
	Girl:	Kim's school is next to Shell Park.
	Man:	How do you spell Shell?
	Girl:	S-H-E-L-L.

4	Girl:	Kim likes me, but I'm not her favourite friend.
	Man:	Who is her favourite friend?
	Girl:	Grace. You spell her name G-R-A-C-E.
	Man:	Do you play tennis with Grace?
	Girl:	Yes, I do.
5	Girl:	Kim plays tennis, too. She's got lots of tennis balls!
	Man:	How many?
	Girl:	Ten. She's got ten tennis balls.
	Man:	Cool!
6	Girl:	Kim has tennis lessons.
	Man:	Oh! What's her tennis teacher's name?
	Girl:	Mrs Bird.
	Man:	Do you spell Bird, B-I-R-D?
	Girl:	Yes! That's right.
7	Girl:	Look at her bag. She's got lots of sports shoes.
	Man:	How many sports shoes has she got?
	Girl:	Six.
	Man:	Six sports shoes! Wow! Great!

Test tip: STARTERS
Listening (Part 2)

✔ In this part of the test, the answers are only names or numbers. The names are always spelled out and come from the Starters word list.

➜ Say some sentences with numbers between *one* and *ten*, e.g. *My house is number eight. (Matt)'s little brother is five. I've got three cats.* Learners listen and write the numbers you say (as figures).

G

Read, draw and colour.

- Put a tennis ball, some football boots and a towel in a sports bag. Show the bag and say *Look! This is my sports bag. What's in my bag? What sports do I like? Let's look in the bag.* Take out an item (e.g. a tennis ball) and show it to the class. Say, e.g. *Oh! A tennis ball! I like ... (tennis)* Ask *What colour is my tennis ball?* Repeat with different items.

- Give learners colouring pens or crayons. Point to the pictures of the bags. Say *Let's read.* Read *Alice loves tennis.* Ask *Which is Alice's bag?* (learners point) Say *She's got her tennis racket* (point to the example picture) *but* (shake your head) *she hasn't got her tennis ball.* Say *Read and draw the things in the bags.*

- Learners read, draw and colour the items in the two bags. Ask different learners *What's this? What sport is it for? What colour is it? Is it Alice's or Matt's?*

Answers

Learners draw the following items:
Blue bag: grey baseball bat and orange baseball cap
Green bag: yellow tennis ball and purple tennis shoes

H

Look, read and write.

- Point to the picture and say *Look at this park. Tell me about it. What sports can you play here?* (tennis, football, skateboarding) *Can you run / ride a bike /play ball / badminton here?* (yes)

- Point to the four lines and say *Write four sports you can play in this park here.* Learners work in pairs and choose four things to write e.g. *football, tennis, baseball, badminton.*

- Learners could also draw their own park and write which sports they enjoy doing there.

7

Let's have fun!

Make a sports poster.

Learners look at SB page 71 Activity 7. Say *Let's have fun! Let's make a sports poster!*

Write *My favourite sport* on the board.

Learners write a list of the clothes and equipment they need. They draw pictures or find them in magazines and cut them out. They stick the pictures on a large piece of paper and label them. They can use the example on SB page 71 as a model.

If possible, learners find photographs of themselves playing the sport and stick them on the poster. They can also include pictures of prizes.

Display the posters if possible.

7

Let's speak!

What do you like? Ask and answer.

Ask different learners *Which sport do you like? Do you like (football)?*

Give each learner a photocopy of '7 What do you like?' (TB page 55).

Point to the pictures along the top of the chart. Say *What are these things?* (basketball, a cake, hockey, a guitar, a cat, a computer, a spider)

Point to the space under the first column and say *Write your name here.* Learners write. Say *Now, look at picture 1. What is it?* (basketball) Ask *Do you like basketball?* Learners reply *Yes, I do. / No, I don't.* Draw a tick on the board and say *Put a tick for 'Yes, I do'.* Draw a cross on the board and say *Or put a cross for 'No, I don't'.* Learners put a tick or a cross. Say *Now, look at all the pictures. What's this?* (a cake) *Do you like eating cake? Put a tick or a cross.* Learners put ticks or crosses.

Say *Tell me about your classmates. Do they like basketball? Eating cake? Spiders?* Point to the spaces under the other columns and say *Write your classmates' names here.* Say *Ask one classmate 'Do you like basketball?' Listen to the answer 'Yes, I do' or 'No, I don't'. Put a tick or a cross.*

Learners ask questions and answer. They complete the chart with names, ticks and crosses.

Home FUN booklet
➜ Pages 18–19 sports
➜ Picture dictionary: sports, places

Go online

to practise your English
to listen to the audio recordings
to find more FUN activities!

8 Not today!

Main topics:	food, animals
Story summary:	Two children are on a shopping trip with their mum. The children want to buy lots of things, but can they find something the whole family will love?
Main grammar:	*and, but, or, Can I/we have …?, Yes, you can. / No, you can't., What's this?, What are these?*
Main vocabulary:	*apple, beautiful, burger, carrots, chicken, chips, donkey, drink, eat, egg, food, fruit, grape, jeans, kiwi, lemon, lots of, Lucy, meatballs, nice, orange, pie, rice, shirt, shorts, sweets, today, tomato, T-shirt, watch*
Value:	Apologising (*"Sorry!"*)
Let's say!:	/f/ /v/
Practice for Starters:	Reading and Writing Part 2 (D), Reading and Writing Part 4 (F), Listening Part 1 (G)

Equipment:	
• audio: Story, Let's say!, E, G, H	• shoe boxes and pretend money, one set per group of three or four learners (optional): C Extension
• (presentation **PLUS**) flashcards (79–114 food): C, H	• bag, pieces of paper with food words from the unit (or flashcards) (optional): D Extension
• (presentation **PLUS**) Image carousel 42–43 (2 pictures of places to shop)	• crayons or colouring pens: C Extension
• shopping bag with food or pictures (optional): oranges, grapes, apples, tomatoes, carrots: Storytelling, C, C Extension	• sweets (optional): H
• shopping bag with clothing or pictures (optional): watch, T-shirt, shorts, jeans, shirt: Storytelling, C Extension	• Photocopy 8 (TB page 56), one per learner, A4 paper, scissors, glue, cardboard tube, crayons or pens: Let's have fun!
	• piece of plain paper (one per learner): Let's speak!

★ ✦ Storytelling

Before listening

With books closed …

- Pick up your bag with food and say *This bag is from a food shop. Let's look in the bag.* Take out an orange and say *Look! What's this?* (learners guess in L1 or English) Say *Well done! It's an orange! Let's look again …* Repeat with different items (grapes, apples, tomatoes and carrots). Ask *What food do you like?* (learners answer)
- Repeat with your bag of clothes: *watch, T-shirt, shorts, jeans* and *shirt*.
- Say *Today's story is about …* (food/clothes/shopping)
- Look at the first picture (with or without the text on the Image carousel or in the book) page 60. Ask *How many children can you see?* (two) *Are they brother and sister? Classmates?* Learners guess.
- Ask *Which shop is this?* (food shop)
- Look at the clothes shop on the Image carousel or in the book pages 61–62. Ask *Which shop is this?* (clothes shop)
- Look at the pet shop on the Image carousel or in the book page 63. Ask *Which shop is this?* (pet shop)
- Say *Now let's listen to the story.* Say *Let's look at page 60.*

Listening

With books open …

22

- Play the audio or read the story. Learners listen.
- Play the audio or read the story again.
- Pause after page 60 and ask *What do Dan and Lucy want?* (some oranges, grapes, apple pie) Point to the trolley and ask *What does Dan put in here?* (oranges)
- Pause after page 61 and ask *What do Lucy and Dan want?* (some meatballs, tomatoes) *What does Mum want?* (carrots) Point to the trolley and ask *Now what does Lucy put in?* (some meatballs)
- Pause after page 62 and ask *What does Lucy want?* (a watch and some shorts) *What does Dan want?* (a T-shirt and some jeans) *What does Mum want?* (two white shirts) Point to the basket. Ask *What does Lucy put in here?* (a watch)
- Play the end of the story and ask *What animals do the children want?* (a snake, a mouse, a fish, a chicken, a donkey) *Which animal goes home with them?* (the donkey)

- Ask in L1 *Do the children help at the shops?* (no) *Tell me about the end of the story. What happens? Do you like the end of the story? Why?*
- Ask *Do you go shopping with your family? Do you like shopping? What do you like buying?*

 Value

- Look at pages 61 and 62. Point to the speech bubbles in bold. Say *Dan and Lucy say …* (Sorry) In L1, ask *Why do they say 'Sorry'?* (Because they did something that made their mum sad/angry).
- Ask *Does Mum feel better when Dan and Lucy say 'Sorry'?* (yes) Say *It's good to say 'Sorry' when you know you are wrong.*
- Personalise the idea of apologising. Ask learners *Do you sometimes say 'Sorry'? When? To who?*

 A **Draw lines.**

- Learners look at the pictures. Say *How many animals can you see?* (four) *What animals can you see?* (a fish, some chickens, a donkey) Point to the pie. Ask *Is this ice cream?* (no) *Is it an apple?* (no) *Is it apple pie?* (yes) Point to the meatballs. Ask *Are these tennis balls?* (no) *Are they meatballs?* (yes) *Do people eat apple pie and meatballs?* (yes) *Do you like this food?* Learners answer.
- Say *Draw lines from the words to the correct picture.*
- Check answers in open class or use Presentation plus.

Answers				
1 d	2 b	3 e	4 a	5 c

 26 | **Let's say!** Student's Book Page 79

Say *Look at page 75. Listen.* Play the audio. Say *Let's say* /f/ **f**rog. Learners repeat. Say *Tell me more English words with* /f/. Learners answer (e.g. food, fruit). Repeat with sound /v/ li**v**ing room (e.g. favourite, have).

 B **Who wants this/these? Write, ask and answer.**

- Learners look at the pictures. Ask *Where's the snake?* (learners point) Repeat for the other pictures, in a different order.
- Read the instructions. Learners write the name of the person who wants each item in the story. They look back at the story to help.
- In pairs, they ask and answer *Who likes …?* questions.

Answers					
1 Dan	**2** Dan	**3** Mum	**4** Lucy	**5** Mum	**6** Dan
7 Lucy	**8** Lucy				

Test tip: STARTERS
Speaking (Part 1)

- ✔ Learners are asked about items in a big picture: *Where's the …? Where are the …?* Learners only need to point to the item. Then the examiner asks the learner to put object cards in various places in the picture: *Put the … in/on/under/between/behind the …*
- → Use a large picture to practise the first part of the test task. Ask *Where's the …? Where are the …?* Learners point. Use small objects, e.g. a rubber, a table tennis ball, a watch, a flower, or use object cards to do the second part of test task. Learners listen to your *Put the …* instruction and place the objects/object cards in the correct place in the picture.

 C **Read and choose the correct answer.**

- Show flashcards of two food items. Say, e.g. *I've got grapes and apples.* Learners repeat. Show two food items. Say, e.g. *I like oranges* (smile), *but I don't like tomatoes* (look disgusted). Learners repeat. Repeat with other pairs of items.
- Say *Read and circle 'and' or 'but'.*
- Check answers using Presentation plus or in open class.

Answers			
2 and	**3** but	**4** but	**5** and

 D **Look and read. Write *yes* or *no*.**

- In pairs, learners look at the picture and write words for things they can see. You could set a time limit. The pair with the most items writes their list on the board. Check spelling: *How do you spell (computer)?*
- Do the examples. Mime eating to teach *eating*.
- Learners read, look at the picture and write *yes* or *no*.
- Check answers in open class (learners put up their hands for 'yes' answers) or use Presentation plus.

Answers					
3 yes	**4** no	**5** no	**6** yes	**7** yes	**8** no

- Stronger learners can correct sentences 2, 4, 5 and 8. (2 Dan is eating fish and chips. 4 The grapes are red. 5 The glasses are on the book. 8 Lucy is eating an apple.)

Extension

Mime eating an apple. Ask *What am I eating?* Learners guess (a pear, an apple). Repeat with different types of food, e.g. a tomato, a burger, a cake, a chicken leg, a banana. Volunteer learners take a food word from a bag and mime eating it for the class to guess.

Test tip: STARTERS
Reading and Writing (Part 2)

- ✔ In Reading and Writing Part 2, the *yes/no* sentences about the picture are usually about numbers, colours, activities, or positions of objects or people.
- → Use pictures in the book or on the Image carousel to practise this task and improve learners' visual literacy. Make sentences, e.g. *You can see three cars. The car is blue. The man is cleaning his car. The car is behind the tree.* Learners answer *yes* or *no*.

E   Listen and tick (✔) the box.

- Say *You are going to listen to some animal noises.* Learners read the animal names.
- Do the example. Ensure learners understand they listen to one of a pair each time.
- Play the audio. Learners listen to the sounds and tick. Play the audio again. Learners check their answers.

23

- Check answers, e.g. *It's a donkey.* (donkey noise)
- Learners can play in pairs. Learner A makes an animal noise. Learner B says the animal. Then swap.

Answers

Learners tick the following animals:
2 a fish   **3** a snake   **4** a frog   **5** a chicken   **6** a dog

Tapescript:

1   (donkey noise)
2   (fish noise)
3   (snake noise)
4   (frog noise)
5   (chicken noise)
6   (dog noise)

F   Read and choose a word. Write.

- In pairs, learners circle the words in the carrot. Check this part of the activity first and write the answers on the board.
- Point to the picture of the donkey and ask *What's this?* (a donkey) Say *It's Dan and Lucy's donkey.*
- Read the first sentence. Show learners that the word *garden* is in the carrot.
- Learners read the text and complete it with words from the first part of the activity.
- Check answers using Presentation plus or in open class. Learners spell the words aloud.

Answers

2 tail   **3** crocodile   **4** water   **5** apples

Extension

Copy these descriptions and display them on the walls of the classroom. Learners walk around, read and guess the animals.
1 *I've got four legs and big ears but I'm not a rabbit. I eat plants. I love playing in water. Do you?*
2 *I've got four legs and a long tail but I'm not a dog. I eat fish. I love mice. I can jump. Can you?*
3 *I haven't got legs but I'm not a snake. I can swim. Can you?*
4 *I've got four legs and a tail but I'm not a cat. I love the sun. I'm green. I can run fast. Can you?*
5 *I've got two legs and a long tail but I'm not a tiger. I can climb trees. I love bananas. Do you?*
6 *I've got two legs but I'm not a girl or a boy. I can make eggs. I've got wings. Have you?*

Answers

1 an elephant   **2** a cat   **3** a fish   **4** a lizard
5 a monkey   **6** a chicken

G   Listen and draw lines.

- Learners look at the picture on Presentation plus or in their books. Ask *What can you find in this shop? You can find … (clothes)* Ask *Where's the dog? Where's the handbag? Where's the chair? Where are the black shoes? Where's the ice cream?* (learners point) Then ask *What's this boy got?* (a banana) *What colour are the boots?* (pink) *What colour is the shirt?* (white) *What colour is the big hat?* (orange) *How many children are there?* (five)
- Practise pronunciation of the names and ask *Is it a girl or a boy?* Say *Pat is a boy's name and a girl's name. Alex is a boy's name and a girl's name too.*
- Play the first part of the audio and do the example. Ask *What has Alex got?* (a hat)

24

- Play the audio. Pause after each section for learners to draw lines. Play the audio once or twice more.
- Check answers in open class or use Presentation plus.

Answers

Learners draw lines as follows:
Sam – girl with pink boots
Pat – girl with handbag
Nick – boy with white shirt

Tapescript:

Boy:	Hi. These are my friends! They're in a clothes shop.
Woman:	Ha ha. Who's that boy? I like his hat!
Boy:	That's Alex. Alex loves hats!

Can you see the line? This is an example.
Now you listen and draw lines.

1	**Woman:**	And who's that girl?
	Boy:	The girl in the cool pink boots?
	Woman:	Yes. I love her glasses!
	Boy:	That's Sam. Sam is her name.

2	**Woman:**	And who's that girl?
	Boy:	Oh, her name's Pat.
	Woman:	Pat's got a nice handbag!
	Boy:	Yes. Pat loves handbags!

3	**Boy:**	And there's Nick. I like Nick! He's funny.
	Woman:	Oh! He's got a white shirt!
	Boy:	Yes. A very big white shirt!
	Woman:	Ha ha. And what's the dog's name? The dog with the sausages!
	Boy:	Ha ha. I don't know.

Listen and sing the song.

- Point to the pictures and ask *What animals can you see?* (snakes, tigers, mice, monkeys) Ask *How many (snakes) can you see?* for each picture. Point to the last picture and ask *How many friends?* (four)

- Review the food in the pictures (cake, burger, rice, kiwi) using flashcards or by drawing on the board. Show some sweets, if possible, to teach *lemon sweets*.

25

- Say *Let's listen!* Play the audio. Learners listen and read. Use gestures to help understanding (e.g. for *Oh no! little, hungry*). Point to the snakes and ask *Where are the cakes?* (learners answer in L1 – in the snakes' tummies) Repeat for the burgers, rice, kiwis and sweets.

- Play the song several times. Learners join in.

- Teach actions for the song, verse by verse:

Six blue cakes! – hold up six fingers

And two long snakes! – move your arm like a snake

Where are the cakes? – raise your shoulders

Oh no! Oh no! – hand in front of your mouth

Sorry! – hands together as if saying sorry

Nine nice burgers! – hold up nine fingers

And three hungry tigers! – make a fierce face and claw hands

Lots of white rice! – mime eating rice with a spoon

And five little mice! – hands on your head like ears

Eight big kiwis! – hold up eight fingers

And four hungry monkeys! – mime a monkey

Ten lemon sweets! – hold up ten fingers

For my friends and me to eat! – point to you and other people

Where are all the sweets? – raise your shoulders

Yum! Yum! Yum! – rub your tummy in a circle three times

- Sing the song with the actions.

Tapescript

See TB page 58

29

- You can also listen to a version of this song without the words for learners to sing along to.

8

Let's have fun!
Make a donkey.

Learners look at SB page 71 Activity 8. Say *Let's have fun! Let's make a donkey!*

Give each learner a photocopy of '8 Make a donkey' (TB page 56), a cardboard tube and glue.

Learners cut out the donkey and use it as a template to cut out another donkey on a separate piece of paper. They colour in the two donkeys and stick them both around the cardboard tube so that it stands up.

Explain in L1 that learners need to draw food for their donkey. Give out pieces of paper. Learners draw items and write the names in English. Circulate and help with vocabulary.

Show learners how to 'feed' their donkey by putting the pictures inside the cardboard tube. Say, e.g. *My donkey likes (carrots).* Learners have fun 'feeding' their donkeys in the same way. Circulate and ask *What does your donkey like?* or *What's his/her favourite food?*

8

Let's speak!

What's on the list? Play a game.

Say *I like fish.* Write *fish* on the board. Ask *What's your favourite food?* (learners answer) *What food do you like?* (learners answer) Say *I like cats.* Write *cats* on the board. Ask *What animal do you like?* (learners answer) Repeat with two more things from the eight stories, e.g. *tennis, guitar, computer, meatballs.*

Say *Look at my list.* After three minutes, rub off the list and ask *Tell me about my list. What's on it?* (learners guess) Say *Yes! Well done* or *No, try again.*

Say *Now you. Write your list. Write ten things you like.* Learners write lists of things they like.

Ask a learner *What's on your list? Do you like cake?* (learner answers *Yes* or *No*) Say *Let's play a game!*

Learners get in pairs. In L1, explain that learners take turns to guess what is on each other's list. Learners guess, e.g. *Apples?* Stronger learners can ask *Do you like …?* or *Have you got …?* questions. The winner is the learner that guesses all ten things first.

Home FUN booklet
➡ **Pages 20–21 food**
➡ **Picture dictionary: food, clothes**

Go online
to practise your English
to listen to the audio recordings
to find more FUN activities!

Counting

1 Help Ben find his shoe. Colour the numbers from 1 to 10.

2 Count and draw lines. Write the numbers.

nine ....

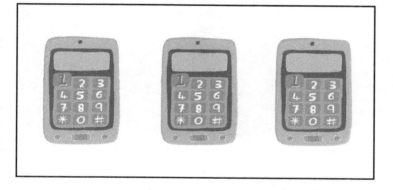

five ....5.........

six ....

three ....

How many?

Cut and play a game.

Come and play with me today

Cut. Ask and answer.

R	L	R	L
D	C	D	C
R	L	R	L
D	C	D	C

The alphabet

4a

1 Write the letters.

a	b	c	……	e	……	g	h
i	……	k	l	……	n	o	……
q	r	……	t	u	v	……	x
y	z						

A	……	C	D	……	F	G	……
……	J	K	……	M	……	O	P
……	R	S	……	U	V	W	……
Y	Z						

2 Draw people you know. Write their names.

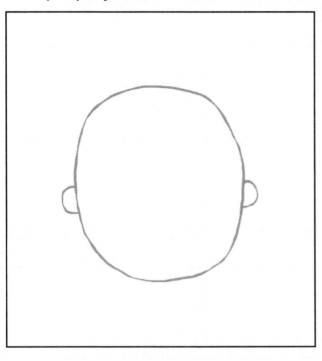

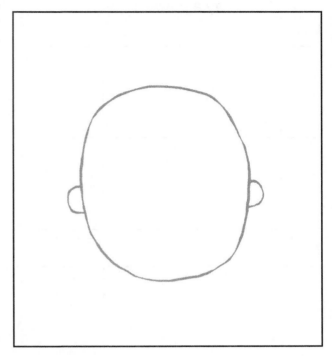

....

....

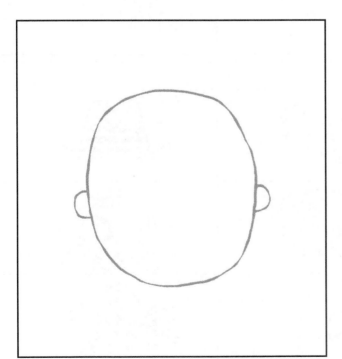

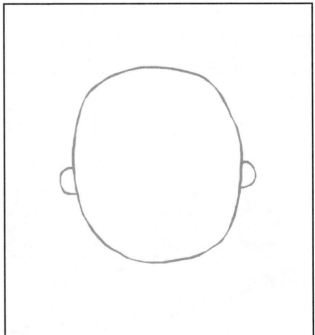

....

....

My name is ....

Bingo!

Cut. Play a game.

1

2

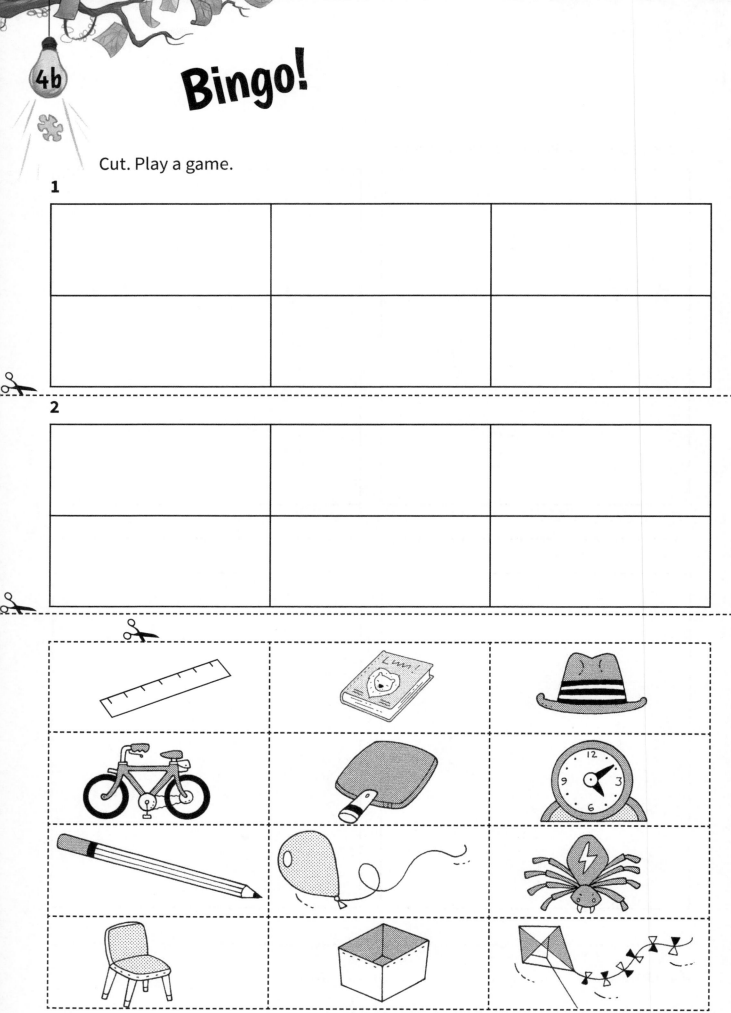

Animals

Draw pictures. Write the words.

....	....	....
....	....	....
....	....	....
....	....	....

Where is it?

Ask and answer. Colour.

  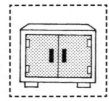 

What do you like?

Ask and answer.

My name's	....	....	....	....	....

Make a donkey

STORYFUN 1

To: ....

(Name of school) ....

(Date) ....

(Signed) ....

Well done!

Song lyrics

Unit 3

It's my birthday today! Hooray! Hooray!
It's a happy, happy, happy, happy day.

Mum and Dad are here. And Jill!
My brother Dan and Grandpa Bill.

Chorus

We've got lemonade and chocolate cake.
And now I'm not seven. Now I'm eight!

Chorus

Thank you, Mum and Dad and Jill.
And thank you, Dan and Grandpa Bill.

Chorus

Unit 4

My school is so cool.
My lessons are great.
How old are my classmates?
We're seven and eight!

My teacher's so cool.
Her name is Miss File.
She's got lots of books
and a really big smile!

Yes, our school's really cool.
Our lessons are GREAT!
Yes, our school's really cool.
Our lessons are GREAT!

Unit 8

Six blue cakes!
And two long snakes!
Where are the cakes?
Oh no! Oh no!
Sorry!

Nine nice burgers!
And three hungry tigers!
Where are the burgers?
Oh no! Oh no!
Sorry!

Lots of white rice!
And five little mice!
Where is the rice?
Oh no! Oh no!
Sorry!

Eight big kiwis!
And four hungry monkeys!
Where are the kiwis?
Oh no! Oh no!
Sorry!

Ten lemon sweets!
For my friends and me to eat!
Where are all the sweets?
Yum! Yum! Yum!

List of flashcards

These flashcards comprise the Cambridge English: Starters test vocabulary list. The unit references listed here are for Storyfun 1. Flashcards can be found on Presentation plus.

1.	bear	36.	hand (U5)
2.	bee	37.	head (U5)
3.	bird	38.	leg (U5)
4.	cat (U2, U5, U8)	39.	mouth (U5)
5.	chicken (U8)	40.	nose (U5)
6.	cow	41.	smile
7.	crocodile (U5, U8)	42.	bag (U4)
8.	dog (U1, U2, U5, U8)	43.	baseball cap (U7)
9.	donkey (U8)	44.	boots
10.	duck (U2, U5)	45.	dress
11.	elephant (U5, U8)	46.	glasses (U6)
12.	fish (U8)	47.	handbag (U6)
13.	frog (U2, U5, U8)	48.	hat (U2)
14.	giraffe	49.	jacket
15.	goat	50.	jeans (U8)
16.	hippo (U5)	51.	shirt (U8)
17.	horse	52.	shoes (U1)
18.	jellyfish	53.	shorts (U8)
19.	lizard (U2, U5)	54.	skirt
20.	monkey (U5, U8)	55.	socks (U6)
21.	mouse (U8)	56.	trousers (U6)
22.	pet (U2)	57.	T-shirt (U8)
23.	polar bear	58.	watch (U8)
24.	sheep	59.	black (U1)
25.	snake (U5, U8)	60.	blue (U1)
26.	spider (U5, U8)	61.	brown (U1)
27.	tiger (U3)	62.	green (U1)
28.	zebra	63.	grey (U1)
29.	arm (U5)	64.	orange (U1)
30.	ears (U5)	65.	pink (U1)
31.	eyes (U5)	66.	purple (U1)
32.	face (U5)	67.	red (U1)
33.	foot (U5)	68.	white (U1)
34.	feet (U5)	69.	yellow (U1)
35.	hair (U5)	70.	baby

71.	boy (U1)	113.	water
72.	brother	114.	watermelon
73.	dad/father (U3)	115.	armchair (U6)
74.	girl (U1)	116.	bath
75.	grandpa/grandfather	117.	bathroom
76.	grandma/grandmother (U3)	118.	bed
77.	mum/mother (U3)	119.	bedroom
78.	sister (U3)	120.	box
79.	apple (U8)	121.	camera
80.	banana	122.	chair
81.	beans	123.	clock (U6)
82.	bread	124.	computer (U6)
83.	burger (U8)	125.	cupboard (U6)
84.	cake (U3)	126.	desk
85.	carrot (U8)	127.	dining room
86.	chicken	128.	door
87.	chips/fries (U8)	129.	flowers (U6)
88.	chocolate	130.	garden
89.	coconut	131.	hall
90.	egg	132.	house
91.	fish	133.	kitchen
92.	grapes (U8)	134.	lamp
93.	ice cream (U3)	135.	living room
94.	juice	136.	mat
95.	kiwi (U8)	137.	mirror
96.	lemon	138.	phone (U1)
97.	lemonade (U3)	139.	picture
98.	lime	140.	radio
99.	mango	141.	rug
100.	meatballs (U8)	142.	sofa (U6)
101.	milk	143.	table (U6)
102.	onion	144.	television/TV (U6)
103.	orange (U8)	145.	tree
104.	peas	146.	wall
105.	pear (U2, U8)	147.	window
106.	pie (U8)	148.	park (U7)
107.	pineapple	149.	playground (U4, U7)
108.	potato	150.	shop (US store) (U7)
109.	rice	151.	street
110.	sausage	152.	zoo
111.	sweets (U8)	153.	board
112.	tomato (U8)	154.	book (U4)

155.	bookcase	197.	throw
156.	crayons (U4)	198.	walk
157.	cross	199.	birthday (party) (U3)
158.	eraser (UK rubber) (U4)	200.	morning
159.	floor	201.	night
160.	keyboard (computer)	202.	alien
161.	mouse (computer)	203.	ball (U2, U3, U7)
162.	painting	204.	balloon (U3)
163.	paper	205.	board game (U3)
164.	pen (U4)	206.	computer game
165.	pencil	207.	doll (U2)
166.	poster	208.	monster (U3)
167.	ruler (U4, U6)	209.	robot (U2)
168.	school	210.	teddy (bear) (U2)
169.	teacher (U4)	211.	boat (U3)
170.	tick	212.	bus (U3)
171.	badminton (U7)	213.	car (U2, U3, U6)
172.	baseball	214.	helicopter (U3)
173.	basketball (U7)	215.	lorry (US truck) (U2, U3)
174.	bat (as sports equipment) (U2, U7)	216.	motorbike (U3)
175.	beach (U7)	217.	plane
176.	bike (U2, U6)	218.	ship (U3)
177.	bounce	219.	train (U3)
178.	catch	220.	sand
179.	draw(ing)	221.	sea
180.	fishing	222.	shell
181.	football (US soccer) (U7)	223.	sun
182.	guitar (U2)		
183.	hockey (U7)		
184.	jump		
185.	kick (v)		
186.	kite (U2)		
187.	piano		
188.	read		
189.	run		
190.	sing		
191.	skateboard (U7)		
192.	skateboarding (U7)		
193.	swim (v) (U7)		
194.	table tennis		
195.	tennis (U7)		
196.	tennis racket (U7)		

Audio track listing

01	Title and copyright
02	Counting
03	Counting D
04	Counting E
05	Counting G
06	Come and play
07	Come and play F
08	Kim's birthday
09	Kim's birthday F
10	Kim's birthday I
11	Hugo's school bag
12	Hugo's school bag D
13	Hugo's school bag F
14	Hugo's school bag I
15	What am I?
16	What am I? F
17	Grandma's glasses
18	Grandma's glasses H
19	Let's go there now!
20	Let's go there now! D
21	Let's go there now! F
22	Not today!
23	Not today! E
24	Not today! G
25	Not today! H
26	Let's say!
27	Kim's birthday song karaoke
28	Hugo's school bag song karaoke
29	Not today! song karaoke

Acknowledgements

The author would like to acknowledge the shared professionalism and FUN she's experienced whilst working with colleagues during 20 years of production of YLE tests. She would also like to thank CUP for their support in the writing of this second edition of Storyfun.
On a personal note, Karen fondly thanks her inspirational story-telling grandfather, and now, three generations later, her sons, Tom and Will, for adding so much creative fun to our continuation of the family story-telling and story-making tradition.

The author and publishers would like to thank the following ELT professionals who commented on the material at different stages of development: Idalia Luz, Portugal; Louise Manicolo, Mexico; Mark Manning, Spain; Alice Soydas, Turkey.

Design and typeset by Wild Apple Design.

Cover design and header artwork by Nicholas Jackson (Astound).

Sound recordings by Hart McLeod, Cambridge.

Music by Mark Fishlock and produced by Ian Harker. Recorded at The Soundhouse Studios, London.

The authors and publishers acknowledge the following sources of copyright material and are grateful for the permissions granted. While every effort has been made, it has not always been possible to identify the sources of all the material used, or to trace all copyright holders. If any omissions are brought to our notice, we will be happy to include the appropriate acknowledgements on reprinting.

The authors and publishers are grateful to the following illustrators:

Marta Alvarez Miguens (Astound) p 57
Andy Elkerton (Sylvie Poggio) p 57
Clive Goodyer pp 47, 48, 52, 53, 54, 55
Kelly Kennedy (Sylvie Poggio) p 57
Melanie Sharp (Sylvie Poggio) p 57
Harriet Stanes (NB Illustration) p 57
Alex Willmore (Astound) pp 46, 47, 51, 57
Gaby Zermeño p 57